'Tween Decks in the 'Seventies

MR SAM NOBLE

'Tween Decks in the 'Seventies

'Seventies

Reminiscences of a Sailor of the Royal Navy During the Victorian Era

By Sam Noble

LEONAUR

'Tween Decks in the 'Seventies
Reminiscences of a Sailor of the Royal Navy During the Victorian Era
by Sam Noble

First published under the title
'Tween Decks in the 'Seventies

Leonaur is an imprint
of Oakpast Ltd

ISBN: 978-0-85706-270-3(hardcover)
ISBN: 978-0-85706-269-7 (softcover)

http://www.leonaur.com

Contents

"SAY, BILL, WOT'S THAT THERE STUFF
YOU'RE ALWAYS A-WRITIN' OF?"
"NOTHIN': ONLY ME LIFE."
"YOUR LIFE! ...YOURN? LOR LUMME! ...
WHY, YOUR LIFE AIN'T INT'RESTIN'."
"AINT IT? ...THAT REMAINS TO BE SEEN, MATE."

OLD LOWER DECK PLAY

TO
JEANIE
MY WEE PILOT

Foreword

It gives me much pleasure to write a foreword to Mr. Sam Noble's engrossing book. In it the Author skilfully depicts life in the Navy of that period in its lights and shadows, though he in his love and loyalty of the Sea Service is a healthy optimist. Above all he shows the great brotherhood of the seaman and rank and file 'tween decks which can hardly be rivalled by the modern comradeship of the Great War.

The greatest maritime power of the world has not yet realised how much it owes to the loyalty, cheerfulness and endurance of the rank and file of the lower deck, not only in recent wars, including the Great War 1914-18, but in times of piping peace.

Think of 1s. 7d. a day for an able seaman, until 1919-20, and as Mr. Noble describes in his book, the four long years of separation, since reduced to two years as a general rule, the coarse fare, the weevilly biscuit in default of bread, and frequently the warfare against wind and weather when sail power was constantly used, the seaman literally at times had to hold on with the agility of a monkey, as everybody who has experienced handling sails on a swaying yard in a rough sea knows to his cost, and the marvel of those old days was that so few men fell overboard to find a watery grave, however the ordeal of the elements stiffened the nerve and sinew of the sailor in a remarkable way only comparable to the ordeal of battle, in which he has fully played his part, as those who will study the naval side of History will admit.

Some reader of Mr. Noble's book may exclaim, "No doubt very fine seamen in his day, but why couldn't a subsequent generation bring off a second Trafalgar instead of an indecisive Battle of Jutland, then we should have had profound faith in the Navy, but now they are second fiddle to the Royal Air Force." The Navy is not surprised at this criticism, however hurt. Briefly, the reply is as follows: "What is the acid test of any victory? The victors remain on the field. So did the British Fleet."

Admitting greater actual losses in numbers on our side of men and ships, and though the German Fleet suffered less severely, thanks to their better protected ships, the moral victory of Jutland was overwhelming, and the spirit of the rank and file of the Navy fostered by their great leaders and traditions of the Navy, which latter has been so clearly and ably explained by Mr. Noble at the beginning of his book—helped considerably towards the greatness of the moral victory of Jutland. Never again did the German Fleet, the pride of the *Kaiser* and hope of the German Nation, endeavour to engage the British Fleet, because their spirit and morale were broken, whereas that of our men was higher than ever.

The Nation, only partially understanding naval warfare, and expecting a spectacular victory, forgot or did not realize the *dictum* of Napoleon, one of the greatest masters of war, who laid it down as a maxim that the moral is to the physical as 3 to 1. We, therefore, achieved a great moral victory at Jutland.

In conclusion, the optimism and bright outlook on life in the Navy as depicted by Mr. Noble still holds good on the whole. I entered the same service ten years after he did, and after forty years in the Navy in peace and war, I can say that the Nation is fortunate in having such a splendid body of men 'tween decks, worthy successors of types in Mr. Noble's book, and it is the duty of the Nation to continue to take interest in their welfare and progress; nothing but the highest efficiency, loyalty and sense of duty for those serving in the Navy will be good enough in the next ordeal by battle. Neglect or be apathetic to the Navy, which is the First Line of Defence and responsible for our Maritime Communications, on which our existence as an Empire depends, and our greatness must decline like the Roman Empire did.

Mr. Noble's book will, I hope, be widely read as it deserves to be, and I hope he may write another.

(Signed) A. P. Davidson, D.S.O.,
Rear Admiral
(Retired),
Royal Navy.

Virginstow,
Devon.

CHAPTER 1

Joining Up

In the year 1875, when trade was bad in Dundee, a few of the youths of our locality, all millworkers like myself, took it into their heads to go and join the Navy, and I went along with them. Personally I didn't dream of joining, being, as I thought, too small (though I loved the sea, and sea-stories were my pet reading), but just went for company. H.M.S. *Unicorn* was then, as she is now, the Receiving Ship. The recruiting-sergeant, a Royal Marine, put them through the catechism, pounded them, weighed and measured them like so many bags of wheat, and then for one fault or another turned them all down.

Seeing me, the sergeant asked if I wanted to join. I said no, I thought I was too little.

He said, "Ah, you're short, my son, but you're stout. Let me try you. How old are you?"

"Sixteen past," I answered.

He then whipped the tape under my armpits, bundled me on to the weighing-machine, stuck me up against the bulwarks under the measuring-rod, gave me a series of thumps on the back, chest and ribs, which sent the breath out of me in little gusts, and finally said:

"You'll do. An inch short, but half-an-inch over chest measurement. I'll make that all right—now look here—"

He then drew such a picture of the sea: how I should have nothing to do but sit and let the wind blow me along; live on plum-pudding and the roast beef of old England; lashings of grog and tobacco; seeing the world the while and meeting and chatting with princesses and all the beautiful ladies of other lands—ah! it was a gay life . . .!

That did the trick! From that moment nothing on earth would suit me better than to be a Jolly Jack Tar. My imagination was fired. My mind was made up. My chums, too, appeared envious of my good

11

fortune. And I had been the only one picked—that was a tremendous feather in my cap! Yes; the sea for me! But it was all so sudden. How would my mother take it?—she would be demented. I spoke this timidly to the sergeant.

"Oh, that's all right, my lad," he said, spreading himself out—and he was a fine-looking man, with his red coat and blue sash and the ribbons at his ear—"you leave your mother to me. Gawd bless her, I'll let her see what her boy will be in a year or two. Never you fear; I'll fix her!"

Then, in case I should cool off, he hurried us all out of the ship and came right home with me.

On the way, it suddenly struck me about my fingers. Some six months previously my right hand had got caught in the wheels of one of the machines I was tending, and the points of two fingers were torn off. I mentioned this to the sergeant.

He pulled up short in the street, examined them and looked blank.

"Ah," he said, "this is bad. Why, the nail of your middle finger is clean gone, and your forefinger is short. . . . Can you move the joints?"

"Yes."

"Do they hurt?"

"No."

"Now, why the mischief didn't I notice this before?" he mused, somewhat disappointed, and a trifle chagrined I thought.

We went on a little way farther and then he brightened up and stopped again.

"Look here," he said, "as I overlooked this, the doctor may do the same. It's a chance, but we'll take it. What you must do is this: When you are asked to show your hands, you twirl the left in front of him for all you're worth, and keep the right in the background. Do you understand?"

"Yes," I answered, smiling.

"Come on, then!"

My mother had the surprise of her life when I returned home ushering in the big soldier. But when he stated his errand there was a terrible scene. No need to dwell upon that. Anybody—any mother at least—can understand what the losing of her only boy would be.

The sergeant had to exert all his powers—and my word they were great! He told her of the money I would be able to send; the fine life

I would lead; the promotion that a boy of my appearance and abilities was sure to win (the villain! he hadn't known me more than an hour!); how I would come back soon, blazing in gold lace and take her to live in a sweet little villa all covered with roses, and look how proud she would be then! How—but why go on? You know the style.

The upshot was that in twenty minutes or so from the time he entered the door, the papers were signed, the Queen's shilling was in my mother's hand, and he had left the house with the strut of a general who has won a battle.

No use going into the days that followed, or the misery of parting—I feel the dull ache of that business even now as I write.—Poets rave about youth being a happy time. . . . It is. But it is also a selfish time—a time that few men win through without hatching some canker that will eat into their souls in after-life.

Had I come across that sergeant of Marines, say, three months after I joined the Navy, I would gladly have stood by and seen him half murdered.

And yet, had I met him eight years thereafter, when the glorious play was over, and the curtain finally rung down, I would have fallen upon his neck and embraced him—might even have kissed him. . . . We are a rum lot!

PORTSMOUTH HARBOUR IN 1875

Thus it was that on a cold, raw morning in September, I was dumped down on the railway station at Portsmouth *en route* for H.M.S. St. *Vincent*.

The journey from Dundee had been wet and miserable, and my companion and I, another boy from the same town, had eaten nothing since we left home the previous night. I remember we had just passed York, and were both standing dejected at the window looking at the grey objects whirling past, when Peter, my mate, who had been to sea before as cabin boy in an Anchor liner, gave tongue to a thought that had been buzzing around in the back of my head for the last half hour. Why not run away and buy some food somewhere? We had both a little money, so that we were sure of one meal at least.

I can't say that I cared for the idea now that it was put into words, for I had a strong desire to be a sailor, and there had been no little trouble at home before I got my desire gratified; and to run away now when I had come this length would look like showing the white feather at the last minute. Besides, I had my mother to think of, and

I knew she would be almost driven crazy when the authorities called upon her, which they were sure to do if I failed to turn up. And the disgrace!

No; I was resolved to stick where I was and trust to luck. But having broached the subject, Peter stuck to it. He told me gruesome tales of the ill-usage boys get at sea—how they were kicked and cuffed and made to work beyond their strength, and half starved. He pictured the grand times we should have roaming about the country at our own sweet will, doing a job here and there, with plenty to eat and nobody to bother us. And I was so hungry that I really believe he would have got me round to his way of thinking if the train hadn't drawn up at Portsmouth, where a head was thrift in at the carriage window and a gruff voice said:

"Hullo, are you from Dundee?"

We answered yes, and were told to "bundle out then, and be quick about it." We did so, and found ourselves in the presence of the ship's corporal (a naval policeman). He was a big, powerfully-built man, black-bearded, with heavy eyebrows of the same colour that met in a bunch right between his eyes and gave his face anything but a gentle look. But he wasn't a bad man at heart, as we soon found out. He ordered us to "come on" very gruffly, but, noticing the wolfish looks we threw towards any baker's shop we passed, he stopped at one and went in and bought four tarts, two of which he handed to each of us, saying:

"Here, yaffle these; you'll have breakfast presently."

What "yaffle" meant we didn't stop to enquire, but fell upon those tarts and polished them off in a way that must have warmed that corporal's heart down to the bottom. I have never forgotten his kind action. Indeed, to this hour I seldom see a tart without thinking of him.

When we reached the harbour and stood waiting the boat, the sun had come out, and the sight around viewed from the pier set my pulses leaping and my heart throbbing with excitement. As a boy I was full of romance. Here, in reality, was the stuff upon which Romance feeds; the embodiment of all in which my imagination had been running riot for years past. The stately ships, with their white and black hulls; tall, tapering masts and snowy sails; the bewildering array of cordage and rigging; the gilded trucks at the mast-heads gleaming like stars; and the commission-pennants streaming away from beneath them like long, white serpents. The guns glinting in the port-holes, and all the windows and brass-work glittering; the boats plying about, and the waves dancing in the light of the morning sun.

There they were, all as large as life, and just as I had seen them in print a hundred times before, the only difference being that they looked a hundred times better in reality than on paper.

All the old songs, too, came back to my mind—"The Red, White and Blue," "Rule Britannia," "Hearts of Oak," "Tom Bowling," "Black-Eyed Susan." My mother used to sing every one of them—and I quivered to think that here, before my eyes, was the source from which they had sprung—that I was, indeed, to become a part of it!

About a quarter of a mile to the left of where we were standing, a large three-decker lay moored fore and aft. Her sails were loosed and hung in festoons from the yards, which at that distance seemed swarming with little moving objects that kept skimming in and out and up and down like white mice.

The corporal nodded towards her and said: "That's your domicile. What d'ye think of her?"

But neither of us spoke. I don't know how Peter felt, but I know that I could not have spoken then to save my life. I was too much wonder-stricken, too full of admiration to let anything of what I was feeling escape in sound, though I have no doubt my face said plenty. I remember the corporal looked at me for a minute, and then I fancied his own softened and he smiled to himself.

Directly in front, almost right in the middle of the harbour, was another three-decker, the *Duke of Wellington*, while close beside her lay the old *Victory*, Nelson's famous flagship—the chief and most glorious of Britain's naval treasures. I was well up in all the stories connected with these immortal names—as what British schoolboy is not? So you may imagine my feelings when I looked upon the old war-worn craft for the first time.

On the left, or Gosport side, were ranged a long line of three-deckers, line-of-battle ships, frigates, and other trophies of the Spanish and French wars, in some places two and three deep, their high poops and fo'c'sle almost shutting out the view of the shore. Those in my time were mostly used as coaling hulks.

The right, or Portsmouth side, was taken up with Government offices, building sheds, towering shears, cranes, and all the paraphernalia of a large naval dockyard; while the piers and jetties were lined with transports and Royal and Admiralty yachts.

The wide expanse of water forming the fairway was teeming with life and bustle—penny steamers darting hither and thither; pinnaces, jolly-boats and cutters, laden with the day's provisions, and pulled along by brawny jack tars bare-footed, in short-sleeved, open-necked jumpers, showing off their hairy arms and breasts brown with exposure under many suns, and with their caps hanging at such an angle on their heads that it was a wonder to me they didn't fall off, who went lumbering and tumbling back to their respective ships, like plump jolly housewives returning from the market.

Trim little gigs, and long snake-like galleys, with the white ensign flying at their sterns, some with officers seated in them, the gold-lace and buttons of their uniforms sparkling when the sun touched them, and manned with supple, swinging figures in blue and white hats and flowing collars, came skimming along cutting the water like cheese-knives, their oars rising and falling with the regularity of pendulums. Water-men's boats, bumboats, pleasure boats, boats of all sorts and rigs, floating bridges and steam tugs, the smoke pouring from their funnels and throwing shadows on the water like long, black whips. A great scene, by jove! for a boy whose life had been spent in a mill.

To crown all, one of the troopships was leaving for India. If I remember rightly, it was the *Euphrates*. She was painted white all over, with the exception of a broad red ribbon which went round her from stern to stern. There were five white troopers, and each had a different coloured stripe to distinguish her. They were the *Crocodile*, yellow; *Jumna*, brown; *Malabar*, black; *Serapis*, green; and *Euphrates*, red.

It must have been a special occasion, or some important personage was aboard, for her yards were manned and a salute was fired as she slowly steamed down the channel. Her bulwarks and rigging were alive with redcoats; and the glint of a feather hat, or the flutter of a skirt here and there, indicating the presence of ladies, added a touch of colour and sentiment to the scene, which was very effective. As she glided along, amid waving of handkerchiefs and resounding "hurrahs," I thought that anything more truly majestic or beautiful surely never was seen in the world. Her figure-head, the Star of India, seemed on fire, and she lay as white and plum on the water as a swan, and carried herself as gracefully, and actually seemed conscious of the admiration she was evoking from all who witnessed her departure.

When abreast of where we were standing, the strains of "The Girl I Left Behind Me" came wafting across to us, and I almost cried with the feelings awakened by the familiar old song. Alas, I, too, had left a girl behind me, and my heart ached as I recalled the sweet hours

I had spent with her before parting. But I thought of the long letters I should be able to write when I was properly settled down, and
the stirring events that would fill them, and there was consolation in
that.

CHAPTER 2

H.M.S. St. Vincent

I cannot recollect what boat took us to the *St. Vincent*, whether it was a waterman's or one belonging to the ship. I think it must have been the former, because the first impression of the boys who were to be my mates would almost certainly have remained with me. Anyway, I remember distinctly that as we rounded the stern, which was full of windows, and had three galleries all ornamented with gold and beautiful carving, the name

ST. VINCENT

printed in large shining letters under the counter, caught my eye, and my blood tingled as all the stirring incidents connected with that famous combination of letters came thronging into my mind. I had a cousin at sea at the time, and the name reminded me of him and of an old song he was fond of singing, especially when he was about "half-seas over." This is how it went:

Oh, what would my old eyes give for to see
Those glorious days again,
When Jarvis true the Span-i-ard slew,
And rolled him in the main,
Bravo boys!
And rolled him in the main!

I knew the name "Jarvis" and the one I was looking at had something to do with each other, although I couldn't strike the connection then. However, I managed to do it afterwards, and was glad to find that it was John Jervis, the great Earl St. Vincent, one of my particular heroes, the man who "soused" the Spaniards so thoroughly at the Cape of that name in 1797.

We pulled up alongside the companion-ladder, and the corporal said: "Now, then."

Mounting this we crossed the gangway and found ourselves in that part of the ship termed "under the half-deck."

Although at that time there were over a thousand boys on board, besides the officers and ship's company, not a soul was to be seen save the ship's corporal of the watch, who was standing at a desk writing. Our guide turned us over to him with the remark:

"Here's another pair of chickens for you, Jimmy. You'll have to feed 'em, though; they're famished," and without more ado disappeared through one of the hatchways communicating with the deck below.

The corporal, without looking up, cried:

"Messenger boy!"

"Sir!" answered a voice from the other side of the deck, and a lad about my own age, dressed in blue, with a bright, open face and curly hair, came running round a cabin-like erection and stopped beside the desk. He stood to "Attention," and saluted:

"Here I am, sir."

"Take these two boys down to the bread-room, and ask the steward to give them a bit of bread and cheese, or something. Now, look lively!"

"Ay, ay, sir."

He signed to us to come along, and led the way through the hatchway used by our former guide. It was a great, yawning hole, with coamings about a foot high. A brass rod ran along the one facing you to hold on by in case you happened to slip going down. This landed us on the lower deck. We then went through another hatchway leading to the Orlop deck; along an alleyway formed by bag-racks on the one hand and a row of cabins on the other, till we came to a door which the messenger pushed open, saying to us, "Come in." This we did and found ourselves in the store where the provisions were kept. A counter faced the door, at the other side of which, in a little cloud of dust, a boy was sorting out a number of flour bags. He looked up as we entered, and said:

"'Allo, nosey, wot's up?"

I almost burst out laughing at this unceremonious greeting, for I thought by the get-up of our escort that he must have been a person of some distinction—an under-officer at the very least. The organ alluded to even helped out that impression. It was of a high, Roman type, and gave an aristocratic touch to his face. However, he didn't appear to notice anything unusual, and merely answered:

"Morning, Dusty," and delivered his message.

"Dusty" (as the bread-room boy is called) was a Cockney, born within the sound of Bow Bells. He rubbed the flour out of his eyes and regarded us a minute while he straightened his back. He then gave his head a derogatory shake and said:

"I see; Scotch, I presoom?"

We said nothing. The smell of the place, suggesting unlimited food, set our mouths watering and flooded our tongues.

"You don't 'appen to know Gen'ral MacClakaty, V.C., of the R'yal 'Oss 'Oosars, do you, my dears?" he continued, spreading his arms along the counter and bowing to Peter and me with great politeness. "'E's a celebrated member, 'e is, and 'is mother takes in our washin'——"

"'Ere, chuck it!" broke in the messenger, in an admiring tone. "No nonsense, now. Come on, 'Jimmy the Fog's' waitin'."

"Is he, my little peacock? Very well," said Dusty, gathering himself up. "But don't ruffle yer pretty feathers. Wot's all the 'urry? There's a long day before us."

Nevertheless, he dived under the counter and fished out a loaf and a basin with some treacle in it. The former he divided into four, and handed a quarter to Peter and me, after gouging a hole in the centre, filling it with treacle and replacing the plug. [1] We soon wolfed our portion, and stood looking hungrily around for more. But none was forthcoming. The messenger then said, "Now, if you're finished"—and out we bundled again. When we got back to the half-deck, the corporal ("Jimmy the Fog" the boys called him), a mild, pleasant-spoken man, entered our names in a big book, measured us again, told us to sit down on a form and wait, and then left us, going into an adjacent cabin. The ship's sides were snow white; the mess tables, stools, traps, and everything sparkling, and the whole place smelling as sweet as a dairy. The great big deck was deserted: nobody at all on it but ourselves. But overhead there seemed to be plenty of life. We could hear loud voices giving orders and hurrying feet, and heavy bodies being moved about, causing a tremendous thumping.

Twice a whole broadside of guns went off—the first so suddenly that Peter and I knocked our heads together. We were still sitting rubbing them when a sergeant of marines stepped briskly up and blew a loud peal on the bugle. We then heard four or five different voices

---

1. This, I may say here, was the usual supper ration served out to us before going to bed, and called "Scoff and Basher."

shout: "Still!" Another order in a lower key was given and a movement made, then—"'Tention! Dismiss!" and down the boys came trooping through the hatchways like a fall of snow.

It was "spelloe"—what is known at school as "minutes."

What a crowd! and of all sorts and sizes—big boys, little boys, fat boys and thin boys; the stream seemed never-ending. They were all dressed in white duck. Some went dancing into the messes and took down their ditty-boxes from shelves running parallel with the edges of the beams; some ran past without taking any notice of us; some merely gave us a glance in the passing and dived into the lower deck; others, again, put their fingers to their noses, made faces at us, and then disappeared, grinning. A dozen or so gathered round the form, and after staring for a minute or two, as if we were creatures from another world, began to joke and skylark as boys do everywhere with new-comers. One asked where we came from; another, "did our mothers know we were out?" a third, with his arms round the necks of the two in front of him, and his head between their shoulders, squinted at us fearfully and squeaked, "Poo' sings!" which set them all laughing.

And so they went on. I see their mischievous faces now.

A few more joined the group, with hunks of bread in their hands, which they were busily eating, and pushed and jostled those behind to such an extent in their eagerness to see what was going on, that the ones in front were almost driven on top of us.

Coming up in the train Peter and I had been discussing the probability of the boys taking their fun over us. I felt sure they would. Peter, with his wider experience of sea life in the Anchor liner, was equally certain, and prophesied a warm reception awaiting us, especially as we happened to be Scotch.

"Ay," he said, "I ken thae Englishers fine. They'll tortur' the life oot o' ye if ye let them. I shouldna' advise ony o' them to meddle wi' me, though; if they dae they'll find they have the wrang soo by the lug."

Looking at him, I thought it very likely. Peter was one of those thin, wiry fellows that can stand any amount of tussling. As for myself, I was small and not of much account. I would have suffered almost anything rather than have quarrelled or fought with them just at the start. But my mind was made up all the same not to stand too much nonsense.

However, so far there was nothing to complain of. They shoved and pushed and wriggled about us; some sat down on the form and squeezed us together; some mimicked our northern accent and laughed—but not very loud, for they knew the corporal wasn't far off, and they were afraid of him, and of a cane, which, I forgot to mention, lay across two brass hooks just above the desk. My cap was knocked off, and when I stooped to pick it up, the boy nearest me on the form stuck a pin about an inch into a very tender spot and caused me to shoot forward so suddenly that my head plunged into the stomach of a boy in front with such force that the shock nearly killed him. I jumped up wild with pain and indignation to catch the one who had jabbed me, but the imp was away along the deck laughing like a hyena. But I knew him again, and I'm glad to say had it out with him by and by. I saw the other one, however, crawl over to the nearest mess and sit doubled up on the stool, and that was some satisfaction.

Peter, too, came in for his full share of the badgering, but I must admit he came through the ordeal with more glory than I did, and, what was better, made good his boast in the train. I sat down again, feeling miserable, and leaning as much to one side as possible, for a pin-stab, as everybody knows, is pretty troublesome. I didn't mind that so much. My feelings were hurt, and I was cold and hungry, and do what I would I couldn't help my eyes filling. This only made things worse. One of them cried:

"Oh, I say, look; 'e's a-going to pipe 'is eye; fetch a swab somebody!"

The words were no sooner out of his mouth than he was pulled back and another boy—a fat, bullet-headed one, took his place and made us an elaborate *salaam*. He chucked Peter under the chin and said:

"Hullo, Joe, 'ave ye come to git yer 'orns clipped?"

"Ay, cud you dae't?" retorted Peter; and before he knew where he was, the fellow got one in the chops that sent him spinning almost out through the entry-port.

The row that followed brought the corporal out of the cabin. He rushed forward and made a grab for the cane, at which the whole tribe disappeared as completely as if a magician's wand had been waved over them.

It would be tedious to detail further my first appearance on the stage of naval life. Let me simply say, then, that shortly after this, Peter and I were taken below and given our first meal at the Government's expense, and did full justice to it. Then we were given a mess number, and a boy was told off to take us round the ship and explain the different parts, and instruct us how to sling and unsling a hammock, and also how to get into it—the crowning event of a most eventful day, and not accomplished till I had a couple of bumps on my head as large as eggs through falling out.

In a day or two my kit was served out, and mighty proud, I tell you, I felt when I put on my new Jolly Jack's uniform. I found, too, that the life was going to suit me "down to the ground," as the saying is, and wouldn't have gone back to the mill—no, not for the price of all the jumble of stone and lime, machinery, jute and all the rest of it in the whole town of Dundee.

CHAPTER 3

What Happened to Nutty

One night a boy named "Nutty" Ford (nicknamed so from the size of his head) caused a diversion in the ship, which included everybody from the commanding officer down. Had the captain been aboard he would have shared in it, too. I heard afterwards that he said he was sorry he had missed it. Nutty was only a few days joined, and had not mastered the way of getting into his hammock. He had got his blanket spread all right, stripped, and was struggling, in a V-shaped position—arms and legs in the air—to get in, when another boy, carrying a paper smeared all over with treacle, came along and, spying Nutty in such a tempting attitude, promptly clapped the paper on his stern and fled. Nutty dropped at once and ran across to the starboard gangway, where Mr. Bennett, the officer of the watch, was waiting to go the rounds. Mr. Bennett was the first lieutenant, known in the training-ship as the commanding officer. He was a perky little gentleman, with the air of a peacock, and an aristocratic mole over his right eye which he was forever fondling. Something of a dandy too, he was, and used a lot of scent. We could always tell when he was about.

Nutty jumped right in front of him, and holding up his nightshirt, cried:

"Oh, please sir, look at this!"

"The devil!" exclaimed Mr. Bennett, giving it a kick. "Hallo! corporal, there! Sound the Assembly!"

In an instant the bugle rang out with a R-r-r-rip! that would have wakened the dead; and then came a scene that would take a better pen than mine to describe in proper fashion. Talk about commotion! The ship was like a pot that has suddenly started to boil, and boil furiously. Boys leaped from their hammocks and flew on deck like the wind, with nothing on but their nightshirts.

There was no time to think about dress, for during the day it was the custom at the first note of the Assembly for the corporals to rush to the ladders with their canes and help the laggards up. What would they do at this time of night having had their sleep or enjoyment broken into?

In less than one minute every boy was on the upper deck in a state of wonder and semi-nudeness. Was it drill? or fire? or some freak of the captain? Nobody could tell.

There were lights on the poop, so aft went the stream. I remember I got a place beside the main bitts, nicely under the lee of the main-mast, a structure as thick as the bole of a big beech, and, gathering my shirt around me, sat there waiting developments.

It was a sharp winter's night, with the moon scurrying through drifting clouds and glancing down only occasionally. Mr. Bennett and Gunner Syme, a tall, heavy man, with a red beard, whose watch on deck it was, were on the poop close to the rail with Nutty between them. There were also three marines carrying ship's lanterns, and one or two corporals. Mr. Bennett ordered the "still" to be sounded, then murmured something to Gunner Syme, who took hold of Nutty, slued him round so that he faced aft, and said:

"Stoop, boy, stoop; up with that shirt. . . . Here!" to the marines, "show a light."

The moment Nutty stooped and the light fell on him the cause of all the hubbub was as clear as daylight. A big black smudge, not un-like the map of Europe, great sluggish rivers oozing out of it, almost covered his breech and went slowly down his legs. The wild shriek of boyish laughter that broke out told that not one of us but knew how it came there.

"Silence!" roared the gunner, taking a piece of rope's-end out of his pocket. "My word! . . . You'll laugh the other side of your mouths presently. . . . Corporals! keep your eyes lifting and grab the first one that makes a sound. . . . D'ye see this?"

"This" was the small piece of rope alluded to, humorously called a "Corrector." It was about eighteen inches long, ending in a wall and crown—a common knot at sea—and as supple as a serpent. Most of the warrant officers carried one, and laid about with it much in the same way as the old schoolmaster used to do with the tawse.

The gunner slowly and impressively twirled his corrector round and round, and I could see Nutty expecting at every turn to feel it come down wallop on his bare buttocks, follow its motions with a fascination that would have been laughable, had laughing not been so risky just then. But, luckily, the gunner had boys of his own. Indeed, at that very minute the carroty locks of one of them could be seen not six feet from where I was crouching, and who could say that he was not the cause of the whole shindy? He was as "tricky" as anybody, and this the father knew, and Nutty accordingly got the benefit.

So he merely twirled his corrector, bending forward and peering into the gloom. When all was quiet again he went on.

"Now boys, what we want to know is this: who put that 'ere treacle on that boy's—?"

Here Mr. Bennett struck in suddenly:

"Teh! tch! tch! tch! Mr. Syme! Don't call it that!"

"Call it, sir!" said the gunner, turning an astonished face to the first lieutenant, "what shall I call it?"

"Oh, not that; that's a hideous word!"

"But . . . why, sir," said Mr. Syme, in a puzzled tone of voice, staring at the object in question, while Mr. Bennett himself looked plainly embarrassed . . . "that's the name, ain't it?"

"I know! I know!" snapped Mr. Bennett, "but it's beastly . . . horrible . . . Call it—er—er—call it—something else!"

"Somethink else. . . . Why, what else, sir?"

"Oh! not that! . . . for goodness' sake not that I" cried the lieutenant, rubbing his mole energetically. "Let's see" . . . considering. . . . "Call it—er—er—call it—er—Bottom! "he jerked out at last.

Oh!" . . . the gunner coughed (but it was mighty like a laugh!)

"Oh! Bottom! . . . ah! . . . very good, sir. But that's not the name *I've* ever heard it called by. However . . . Now, boys," he cried, sharply turning to us—it seemed to me for relief—"who put that 'ere treacle on that boy's—bottom? Come on now; out with it!"

It was a great sight the moon threw her silvery eye upon as she fitfully peeped from under the drifting clouds while the proper name for a boy's nether regions was being debated. Over the bridge of years how clearly it all comes back! The great ship with its huge spars and network of rigging standing ghostly in the gloom; the group on the poop with the lights twinkling, and poor Nutty among them with his shirt-tail flapping in the wind, and the treacle slowly running down his legs; and all of us boys filling the big, dark deck with our half-clad bodies, and the air with the sound of our chattering teeth; the gunner scratching his head and twirling the corrector; the lieutenant rubbing his mole, and the expressions on the different faces as a passing ray from the lanterns flashed them for a moment into view—all this was as funny as a scene in a pantomime.

But you daren't laugh!

"Come on," cried the gunner; "who did it? Now, then ... own up! ... Mind you, I'll find out!"

There was a deep silence. Everybody thought about his neighbour, but nobody spoke. Cold though I was, I felt a tingle go through me that kept me warm. What must the boy have felt who did the deed?

Mr. Bennett muttered something again to Mr. Syme and the gunner held up his hand.

"Now look here," he said, insinuatingly. "The commanding officer promises that if the boy owns up, nothing will be said to him. . . . Now, then. . . . Come along; don't keep us here all night."

No answer. The boy evidently thought that though nothing was to be *said* to him, something might quite possibly be *done*. So he held his peace. The ship was as quiet as a dead-house; even the teeth- chattering stopped.

"D'ye hear?" roared the gunner, now losing all patience, but wishful to make another appeal. "D'ye understand Mr. Bennett's offer? . . . which, I think, is a very fair one. ... If the boy owns up, not one word will be said to him. . . . If he don't . . . and I find him out . . . !" he growled and slapped his leg.

Not a sound!

I felt that warm tingle go down my spine again. How I envied that boy! They most assuredly couldn't catch him; he had done his job too well.

That seemed to be the officers' opinion also, for after a short pause, during which they conferred together, Mr. Syme said very impressively:

"I've a good mind to keep you all here an hour. . . . But wait . . . I'll catch him. . . . pipe down!"

He then gave Nutty one stinging swipe with the corrector, which sent him off with a bound. In another minute the decks were cleared and we were all turned in again, with the corporals prowling under our hammocks hoping to find somebody talking. But they didn't find me.

In the morning I had forgotten all about it. In a day or two it was common property that the plaster had been applied by Peterswiel, an imp from Ipswich, who joined about the same time as myself. But, of course, nobody ever dreamt of giving him away.

Chapter 4

The Fight for the Pork

Before I was a month in the ship I had my first fight and, luckily, got the best of it. I was in 34 Mess on the lower deck. The caterer was a Cockney, named White, a tall, lanky youth, with a complexion like a tallow candle, and a conceit that sickened everybody. He bullied me unmercifully, and made me do lots of the dirty work of the mess that I had no right to do, besides forcing me to wait upon him hand and foot. If I made the least mistake in anything he would give me a clip on the side of the head, or a kick out of his way, and call me a "Scotch pig!" I had to sit at the bottom of the table and see novices who had joined later pushed ahead of me, while if I said anything, he would mimic my words and hold me up to the ridicule of the whole mess. As there were 22 in it, and I the only Scotch boy among them, it will easily be seen that there wasn't much sympathy for me. Although, I will say, none of the others tormented me as he did.

How I hated the brute! and how I chafed in secret at his treatment. But my salvation was to be worked out in a way neither he nor I expected.

We were allowed a quarter-pound of pork every morning for breakfast; but all the time I had been in the ship I had never managed to be down below soon enough to get my share. There was so much to do and White was such a cad that he would not let me off anything. So I was generally late, and had to content myself with whatever leavings there was of bread and a splash of cold cocoa in the bottom of the mess-kettle. There were usually some outside parings of pork left, but they looked so green and dirty with much handling that I could never stomach them. I used to look with envious eyes at the head of the table where White sat with his chums faring sumptuously on the fine, lean meat, and think what a selfish beast he was.

It happened that a Scotch boy was caterer of 31 Mess, on the starboard side of the deck. He had the reputation of being the second-best fighter in the ship. A big, swarthy, pock-marked fellow he was. He accosted me on the night I joined, and asked if it were true that my name was Noble, and that I came from Dundee?

I said it was.

"So do I," said he. "And my name's Noble, too. Jimmy Noble—say, I'm your cousin."

He then informed me of what he could do in the fighting line, and that he meant to look after me; for which, being a small chap, I was very grateful. He finished up by asking if I had any money? I said I had—three and sixpence.

"That's right," he said. "You give it to me in case you lose it. I'll look after it for you."

I did so; but he must have forgotten all about it, for I never saw anything of it again.

Well, one morning, coming down later than usual, and finding nothing but a piece of green fat and the heel of a loaf for me, I took it over to let Jimmy see it. Jimmy himself was sitting at the time with a tempting display before him. I was just at the crying point with vexation and hunger. He got me to sit down beside him and gave me a piece off his plate and some warm cocoa, telling me to "tuck in," and he would let me know what to do later on.

How I enjoyed that breakfast! It was the first decent meal I'd had since I came aboard.

After divisions, we went to a quiet corner, where he explained how I was to set about bettering things. He said I must fight for it. All the boys had to—Scotch boys especially.

"Look here," said he, "I'll tell you what you'll do. . . . Tomorrow, if you get stuff like you had today, you go up the table and fling it in White's face and take his. . . . Now, mind you do it," he added, quickly, seeing the look of dismay that came into my face on hearing this— "mind you do it, or you'll get a hiding from me." The vicious nip he gave my arm told me he would, too.

I was now between two fires, and almost certain of a scorching from one or other of them. All through the forenoon I thought and thought, but saw no way out of the difficulty and passed the day miserably.

Next morning I came down and found the same mass of green blubber awaiting me. Instinctively I looked across the deck to Jimmy.

He was alert! He threw over a half-threatening, half-encouraging nod, and I saw his lips form the words, "Go on!" There was nothing else for it.

With an inward prayer to heaven for strength and a good aim, I sidled up the gangway between our mess and the next, and before those at the top could recover from their astonishment at a novice taking such a liberty, I let fly, and the greasy missile struck White fair between the eyes, filling both of them. I then snatched the pork from his plate—a fine, square, juicy, lean bit—and into my mouth it went.

White let a yell out of him, and scraping the fat from his face flung it into the boy's opposite. In a moment all was confusion. I had scarcely swallowed the pork when I found myself standing up to White, and he dancing round me like an India-rubber man.

How I got through the next ten minutes goodness only knows. I was knocked down in the first round; had my ear peeled in the second; and in the third I got such a drive in the stomach that the nugget I had bolted jumped back into my gullet again and almost choked me.

But I had drawn blood. White's nose was bleeding, and when the shout went up, "First claret for Scottie!" I tell you my heart sang! And I remember thinking: "What fine sports these English fellows are!"

In the fourth round Providence very kindly placed White's legs against the coamings of a hatchway. I gave him a clean hit, and down he went into the deck below like a sack of potatoes. Two of his chums brought him up again in no time, but he had had enough of it. He held out his hand and "gave me best."

From that morning I had no trouble whatever. No more fagging, and breakfast always kept—a nice piece of fine lean pork on a plate, bread to correspond, and cocoa warm—all waiting for me when I came down. I had any amount of help and tips given me, too, so as to get my things done and be down in time to enjoy the meal. After all, Jimmy's advice, not to mention the other little kindnesses he did for me, was not dear at three and six.

CHAPTER 5

Scrap No. 2

I was only about seven or eight weeks in 34 Mess when I was shifted to 24, on the middle deck, among the Petty Officer boys. This mess
was the Park Lane of the *St. Vincent*: the P.O. boys being considered—
or considering themselves, which is the same thing—the aristocracy
of the ship. The reason for my early promotion was that I soon learnt
to use the "bo'sun's call"—that is, the whistle for regulating drill—and
was lucky enough to attract the attention of Mr. Phillips, the chief
boatswain, who promised to speak to the captain, and get me made a
bo'sun's mate-boy.

Accordingly, one day I was sent for by the mess corporal, and told
to get my bag and in future to stow it in the rack belonging to 24
Mess on the middle deck.

Here another rumpus took place. As I have said, 24 was the Petty
Officer boys' mess, the "upper circle" of the *St. Vincent*, and I was not a
Petty Officer boy—was merely a novice, in fact. The caterer, a slim slip
of a lad, named Browning, belonging to Houndsditch, London, was a
Greenwich school boy, and as full of pride as a young bantam.

Those Greenwich school boys, being trained in seamanship before
joining the Navy, easily outran their mates and won distinction early.
That made them a bit cocky as a rule. There were two of them in
24: Browning, and another London boy, Charlie Caiman by name,
a bright-faced, sweet-natured lad, who was further distinguished by
having an uncle who was a Beefeater in the Tower. This latter boy,
Charlie, and I became chums afterwards, and I spent two or three gorgeous weekends with him at his home in the Minories, and roaming
wild among the gloomy dungeons in that grim old fortress.

Nice enough fellows they were, those Petty Officer boys I mean;
you found them so after you had *impressed your* niceness on them in

the old, old boy way, by knocking it into them. Not that *I* was much of a fighter. Never was. But neither were the boys I happened to be up against. And luck was usually with me—a tremendous asset in a boxing bout.

However, I did as I was told: put my bag and ditty-box alongside of the aristocrats, and went through the forenoon's drill and lessons with a heart as light and as high as the pennant at the masthead.

At dinnertime, my first meal in the mess—(I remember it was "Sea pie" day and the deck was full of delicious flavours)—I hung around rather diffidently till all the others were lined up, not wishing to be thought cheeky; and then, seeing a vacant place about the middle of the table, lifted my leg over the stool and stood waiting for "Grace" to be said.

It was amusing to hear "Grace" said at dinnertime—the only meal, by the way, that was considered worthy of such a distinction. This was quite a ceremony, often a very trying one. The "still" was sounded; then the officer of the deck (there were two mess-decks in the St. Vincent) walked slowly round the messes, where the boys were lined up, each in front of his plate, asking as he passed: "Any complaints? All right here?" etc., etc. Then, having made the circuit of the deck, and got back to the main hatchway where he started, he would wait for his opposite number either above or below to arrive. Sometimes there would be a hitch somewhere, and then we all had to wait, as a rule ravenously hungry with the flavour of the dinner filling our noses, and making our mouths water, till the hitch was adjusted. You daren't take a bit on the sly, for if you did, and got caught!

I had a mate called Archie Smith, belonging to Perth, who once sneaked a nugget of Christmas pudding, and had just plunked it boiling hot into his mouth when the captain and officers came along. He daren't chew—that would have given him away—so he bolted the hunk whole, feeling it scorch his gullet all the way down. But never a murmur! Eyes front all the time! It set up some trouble that was the means of his being invalided, and eventually carried him off altogether—not very long afterwards, either, poor chap.

Sometimes, when the flavour was special, or Mr. Bennett was in a particularly good mood, he would rub his knob with a pleased twinkle in his eye, and preach us a little homily on how grateful we should be for having such nice grub to eat, and what a grand profession the Navy was, and what a fine country we lived in, and a lot of balderdash like that, while we, with the slaver running down our chins, stood squinting at our plates. Then he would shout:

"Say Grace!"

and a thousand boys would immediately yell:

"What we are about to receive may the Lord double it!" In less than five minutes every plate would be emptied! Of course, the correct "Grace" was:

"*For what we are about to receive may the Lord make us truly thankful,*" but we hadn't time for all that.

This day, however, I wasn't interested in the "Grace" or the dinner either. As I took my place they all looked at me, but nobody spoke. I saw the fellow at the top of the table next Browning give him a nudge, which he answered by a nod and a jerk of the head in the direction of Mr. Bennett, who was starting on his round of inspection, and a meaning glance passed between him and the fellow opposite.

I thought it was all right; that the caterer knew of my coming and had the place kept for me. But I was mistaken. When "Grace" was said, and I made to sit down, the fellows at the top and bottom of the stool jerked it back, and down I went with a bang that almost rattled my bones out through my skin, and nearly knocked my brains out besides with the bump I gave my head on the stool. In my descent I grabbed the table cover and brought half-a-dozen dinners along with me, broke the plates, and scattered the grub all over the deck.

The mess was the first one forward, next to the sick bay, and there was a wide gangway between it and the bulkhead. Many a time we danced in it when the band played 'tween decks during the officers' dinner hour.

But it was a different dance this time.

I got up dazed, not knowing whether it was Christmas or Easter, and felt myself all over. Then, collecting my wits, I made a dive at the fellow at the top of the table, Ikey Bean, by name, who wasn't expecting me, and landed him right on the nose—a fine, soft, juicy nose it was, too!—and he had blood for dinner that day, I can tell you. Down he went. Then I rushed for the one at the foot; but he wouldn't stand—sprang right out of my way he did, and got mixed up with the mess-gear—so I took the first that came and, with a lightning punch in his empty stomach, he followed Ikey.

Then arrived Pandemonium!

In the turmoil I heard Browning's voice say:" Leave him to me," and there was I in a whirling circle of excitement sparring up to him

33

like a windmill. He let fly, and got me on the side of the neck—a blow that sent me careering up against the sick bay with a force that nearly put me into it. But I bounced off again, and at it we went, hammer and tongs, with the whole middle deck and part of the lower as spectators.

Browning was about my own size and weight, but he had the advantage of me in his bouts with the Greenwich schoolboys; and I believe would have handled me roughly had luck not come my way as it did in my first scrap.

In one of his plunges he stepped on a potato, and his heel slid about four feet throwing him off his balance. His arms went up and he came down with his head thrown back, like an acrobat doing a leg-stretching feat on the stage, and with all his guard open. Seizing the chance, I flew at him and got one in under his chin that sent him rolling into the corner like a ball.

I looked wildly around to see who was coming next, but just then a cry of "Wa-a-re-o" behind, like the long quivering note of the loon, signalled the arrival of the corporals with their canes, and the crowd vanished like smoke in a wind. Next minute it seemed an octopus had gripped me. It was Tubby Molgan, the mess corporal. Tubby was a little round barrel of a man, with a greedy-eyed, hairy, rat face, and the strength of a gorilla. He was also punishment corporal. It was he who lugged the defaulters up before the skipper, and if anybody had a dozen with the cane or the birch ladled out to him, it was Tubby who laid them on. He nearly squeezed my life out. Then he jerked my head up so that he could see my face, and gave a great start.

"Hallo!" he exclaimed, "why, you're the boy I sent here this morning, aren't you?" I let my head drop as if it had the weight of a mountain. "What's the meaning of this?" he cried, facing round. "Where's the caterer of the mess?"

Browning, who had unrolled himself, and looked a proper battle-scarred veteran, came crawling over, with his head in his hands as if he were holding it on, and said, "Here, sir."

"Oh, you're there; are you?" said Tubby, his harsh, menacing voice like a dog's growl. "And what's the meaning of this 'ere? What have you done to this boy? I sent him here this morning by the express order of the Captain and Mr. Phillips; and now look at him. . . ."

Browning mumbled that it was all the result of a joke. That it was merely intended I should pay my footing as a new member . . . but His voice trailed away to a wheeze, and he put up a weary hand and lifted his head a bit and looked at the corporal.

Tubby was furious. A joke! By heavens, a capital joke. . . . Browning had no idea! . . . He would see what sort of joke it was before he (Tubby) was done with him! That he would! . . "Here's a pretty picture!" he fumed. (I agreed with him. It *was* a lovely picture of a battlefield. Beef, duff, potatoes, onions, and all the other savoury ingredients of sea pie trodden into the deck. Knives, forks, broken crockery, and what not, strewn all over. Ikey Bean's blood, which had flowed freely—rich, thick blobs of bright crimson—adding a lovely realistic touch suggesting *carnage*. Caiman told me afterwards that he envied me my luck in bringing it about.) "Here's a fine state of things," cried Tubby, bending his heavy beetling brows upon Browning in a terrible frown. "You are supposed to set an example to the other messes and look at this! . . . Whoever saw such a mix-up? And you call it a joke! . . . We'll see what the Captain has got to say about it."

He brought the whole mess out amidships, whipped out his notebook and took every one of our names, bullied everybody, threatened Browning with disrating, ordered the mess to be scrubbed out, and dared one of us to so much as put a crumb in his mouth till he gave permission—kicked up a proper shindy, in fact, and then went off in a blaze of fireworks.

Such a how-de-do!

The first thing Browning did when Tubby was out of sight was to hold his hand out to me, which proved him a thoroughbred, and made me love him. I gripped it heartily, and one of the fellows on the starboard side cried, "Bully for Browning!" which raised a small cheer; but this was soon doused by Jimmy-the-Fog at the desk, who held up both his hands, crying "Hush!"

Then we all set to work to get things into shipshape order again. It was "off jumpers, up trouser-legs." Some rushed to the galley for buckets of warm water, others for brushes, squeegees and swabs. Caiman ran to his ditty-box and fished out a big hunk of soap, and into the work we went "like brothers in a common cause," and all enmity forgotten. By the time Tubby came to inspect the mess you wouldn't have known anything had happened, beyond the deck being wet and some of our faces a bit askew.

After the inspection we had another thriller. Browning stepped up to the corporal as he was going away and asked permission to say a word. Tubby said: "What was it?" frowning like an angry chimpanzee. Browning said he was sorry for the row, also for the trouble it had caused, but he hoped the corporal would be kind enough not to report his messmates, as they had nothing to do with it; the blame was all his, and he was willing to bear the consequences.

Tubby flowered at him with his hang-dog face, gave a shrug to his shoulders, saying: "That's for the captain to settle"; threw a scowl around, which took us all in, and departed, growling in his beard.

A proper curmudgeon.

But we all thought it grand of Browning. It showed him a true sport. Down we sat to what was left of the dinner, as cosy as peas in a pod, eating it as happily as though it had been the finest fare in the world, instead of cold, tasteless hash—very little of it, too, and some even trampled. I couldn't help smiling over to him in an admiring sort of way as he sat at the head of the table, and he smiled back, telling me there was no ill feeling. The whole crowd were as decent as could be, some giving me bits off their plate though they hadn't much for themselves. Ikey sat opposite; and though his nose was a bit lumpy and high-coloured from the bash it got, geniality flowed from his eye. Charlie Caiman threw me a grin which warmed my cockles, and was the start of a chumship which lasted all the time we were in the *St. Vincent* together, and afterwards, and would flame up as brightly as ever in a moment should we happen to meet one another again. My left eye was bunged up, my neck twisted, and my tongue bitten through; but the day was mine, and I felt like an admiral back from a tough, totally unexpected engagement "with all his blushing honours thick upon him," and hugged myself to think I had got off so easily.

I don't know what happened—perhaps Mr. Phillips heard of the racket and put in a word—but nothing more was said about it. After that, things went as smoothly as clockwork.

Browning, poor fellow, shortly afterwards was drafted to the *Eurydice*, and went down in her on that fateful day in March, 1876.

Altogether my days in the *St. Vincent* slid along as happy and full of events as even a boy could wish. I was eighteen months aboard of her, and "passed out" of my classes creditably. The days were employed in instruction in everything that can make a man useful, the evenings in play or study, or writing home. I loved the life, and was ever so glad now that I had left the mill. This was a life really worth living. There was a flavour and tang about it as sweet as the sea itself. It was full of Interest. Full of Adventure. Full of Possibility. Full of Change. You never knew where you would be sent, or how soon.

Whereas the mill . . .!

Coming back one day from the pier after landing an officer (I was in the gig's crew) Charlie Caiman met me with the news that we were both drafted to the *Victory*. That is an event I remember well. At the time, the dearest wish of my life was to be sent there, and I recollect that the sudden realisation of it nearly dropped me. I thought Charlie was joking. But he wasn't. In twenty minutes from the time he told me, we were in the boat rounding the stern of the "Saint," and waving farewells to some fellows at drill on the mizzen. And that is the last recollection I have of her. We hadn't time to say "Goodbye" to anybody. But, of course, they would all know.

That's always the way in Andrew Millar.

No delay. Ready, aye ready!

CHAPTER 6

H.M.S. Victory

The *Victory* was a cushie job—plenty to eat and nothing much to do. Boys were sent to her for signal instructions, but her old, glorious days of usefulness were done, and she was now a show ship. I soon familiarized myself with every stick and rope-yarn aboard of her, and, having read Southey's *Life of Nelson*, found the old ship absolutely IT in the way of interest. Nelson, too, was my pet particular hero, and everything around and about spoke something concerning him. A picture of the Admiral hung on a bulk-head under the half-deck thrilled me the moment I stepped aboard. I got to know that picture by heart, every line and shade of it, before I was done with the *Victory*. I'll tell you how presently.

All about the old ship was interesting, to me fascinating. Here, for instance, on the quarter-deck, was the spot where Nelson fell—on the yet wet blood of his poor secretary. Here, on the poop, the place where the two midshipmen stood while they plugged the fellow in the *Redoubtable's* mizzen-top who had shot him. Here, the point where, being carried below, mortally wounded, the Admiral noticed that the tiller-ropes, which had been carried away, were still unrepaired, and ordered them to be seen to. Here, marked by another plate, the spot where, nestling in the loving arms of Captain Hardy, his friend, he died. I never looked at this place in the cockpit—and I came to it many a time, and lay full length on the very planks Nelson's body had covered—all the boys did it—but another scene, illustrating my hero's staunch spirit to the end, came back to me.

He had asked Captain Hardy to anchor after the battle, and Hardy had answered that Admiral Collingwood would take over the command of the fleet, when Nelson, trying to raise himself, said: "Not while I live, Hardy!" and fell back again.

Here, in the cabin, was the table on which he wrote his very last letter—that one asking the country to protect Lady Hamilton. Here, triced up and spread out with the shot-holes showing, were the old Trafalgar sails; here, one of the shot-holes through the hull, plugged up, of course, but kept char of whitewash for visitors to see; here this, here that—interest everywhere!

I hauled Charlie Caiman about with me, and we devoured it together with the relish of little dogs worrying liver. We snipped a small piece out of one of the sails, and cut off one of the reef-points as trophies to bring home. Mine I gave to a girl years afterwards. Had I known this literary stunt was to come, wouldn't I have kept these and other relics I brought back from sea with me!

The *Victory* at this time was commanded by an officer named Farroll, a tall, grave, dignified gentleman, who wore one gold ring on his sleeve, like a sub-lieutenant's, but without the curl. He had been a blue-jacket at one time, so I heard, and was the only man in the service permitted to wear that mark of rank. We boys called him "Father" Farroll, on account of his gentle ways.

He paced the quarter-deck, or went through the ship bent slightly forward, with his hands clasped behind his back, seemingly always in thought, and never noticed any of us. But just you get taken up before him . . . Then he made you squirm! Not that he was harsh or loud-voiced, or his punishments severe, but his words had the knack of going straight to the mark, and working inside of you like a fizzy drink.

Who the other officers were I don't remember; while among the ship's company—which was small compared with the *St. Vincent*—the only outstanding figure I recall is a man named Moss, a ship's corporal.

I remember him well.

The reason I do so is because of an incident which he and I had the fortune to share together. I don't know how it affected him, but I know it was the means of stamping that man's individuality upon my memory in a way that put it beyond the possibility of ever being rubbed out.

You'll hear all about this, too, in a minute. He was one of the biggest men I ever saw—tall, large-boned, broad-shouldered, hairy-breasted—I used to admire him as he washed himself of a morning—clean-shaven, with the jowl of a prize fighter.

But for all he was big and gruff-looking, Moss was a rare good sort. He was a fine bass singer, and usually sang songs with good-going choruses, such as "Pour out the Rhine Wine," "Nancy Lee," or "While the Foaming Billows Roll," which everybody knew and loved to join in. He would go through the verse himself, and then we youngsters would chime in with the chorus, and make the ship ring with our fresh, shrill voices. These are treats I often recall and savour again now when I'm an old man: especially one night while he was singing, when he looked across the deck and saw me almost bursting myself in the chorus, and smiled over to me. I believe that smile stood me in good stead when I got into his black books.

One of Corporal Moss's best was "The British Lion." I have never heard it sung since I left the Service, but many a time it has cheered me at my work, or when skimming along a country road on my little machine during the years that have gone.

It went this way—of course, I quote from memory:

Oh, the British Lion is a noble scion,
And proud of his conscious might,
A terror to those he has made his foes,
But he ever defends the right;
And so meek and mild that a tiny child
May approach him and never quail,
And may pat him on the crown, and stroke him down,
But beware how you tread on his tail!

The last two lines were repeated as chorus.

To see Corporal Moss while he sang this song was to get an idea of how the present greatness and glory of Britain have come about. Standing like a rock, his chest expanded, shoulders square, head thrown back, his eye glowing with patriotic fervour, his deep voice pealing out, every note as clear and vibrant as if coming from a 'cello; and every word like the stroke of a bell, and his whole manner and bearing expressing the title of his song—by Jove! I tell you that was a sight worth going miles to see. He looked the very picture of Noble Defiance—as if he could have stopped an army himself.

One night I particularly remember. We boys were playing about the fore part of the ship and on the fo'c'sle, the P.O.'s and ship's company being farther aft in the waist. It was a fine night with no wind, and that strange hush which nature throws over those spring nights and makes sound travel so far, especially on the water. Suddenly Moss's voice rang out like the sound of a trumpet and stopped the play. Away went the notes, reverberating along the deck, mounting into the rigging, gambolling and dancing among the masts and spars like elves in a wood, thrilling everybody that heard them.

The song was very popular at the time. Everybody knew it. At the end of the eight lines we took up the chorus, and the men of *The Duke* (which was anchored close by) who had been listening, *they* took it up also and

> *You may pat him on the crown and stroke him down,*
> *But beware how you tread on his tail!*

went rattling up Pompey harbour and into the town like a presage of still greater glories to come.

When the chorus finished we boys looked at one another, grinning and shaking our heads as much as to say, "What do you think of that? Let them try it!"

I didn't make much headway at signals, and I hated school. The schoolmaster's name was Mr. Rabbits. I remember it because I got into a row the first day I was at school for calling him "Mr. Hares": one of the other boys told me that was his name.

What I particularly liked was showing visitors round. Hundreds of them came—princes, peers, lords, ladies—all sorts and conditions of people to pay their respects to the little hero of Trafalgar—My Hero!

When a party arrived, if it happened to be make-and-mend-clothes day, when we were all free, one of the boys would shout "Keb!" (meaning cabby, or conductor) and there would be a rush to see if the crowd was a likely one; *i.e.*, good for a tip; if not, it was left severely alone, and anyone could take it that liked. Sometimes this reasoning didn't turn out sound, for a most unlikely lot often proved a good investment.

One of the boys, who came from the *Impregnable*, had a poem in MS. in his ditty-box, purporting to have been written by a man who had served in the *Victory* at Trafalgar. He showed it to me and I "took it in" at once. At that time I could memorise poetry that interested me at the first reading, and reel it off word for word when wanted, like a gramophone.

This piece was pretty long, forty verses or thereabouts as near as I can remember, and the writer must have been an even greater admirer of Nelson than myself, for his hero's name occurred at least thirty times throughout the poem—sometimes twice in one verse; once, I give you my word, actually four times in as many lines.

Here is the verse—the others have mostly escaped my memory, the few I have retained have kept the grip by reason of their very uniqueness:

> *Beloved Nelson! there you lie,*
> *True-hearted Nelson! England's pet,*
> *Ah, Nelson's name will never die,*
> *Brave Nelson's sun will never set.*

Poor stuff, no doubt; but you have no idea how effective when declaimed to the yokels and farmers who came in shoals from up country. You should have seen them lick their lips and nudge each other over it. Once, a countryman with a rich, rolling Devonshire accent, said to me:

"Who wrote that lovely poetry, master?"

"I couldn't tell you his name, nor where he belonged to," I answered, "supposed to be a seaman who was in the ship with Nelson when he died."

"This 'ere ship?"

"Yes."

"My! he were a clever 'un, master! Don't 'e think so? It's grand, bean't it?"

"It is so!" I agreed heartily, and really thought so, think so still. I've read worse from poets of much higher pretensions.

I collected over half a sovereign from the crowd that young fellow belonged to—bless 'em! —and it came in very handy. A nice little addition to my weekly sixpence. I sent two thirds of it to my mother in Dundee, who always shared my joy—and the spoil.

The piece described the battle, Nelson's death and the manner of it; took you right through the ship, touching on every point of interest as you passed and ended in rhapsody.

For instance, at the brass plate on the quarter deck this verse occurred:

> *On this fair spot which now you see,*
> *Fell one of Britain's heroes bold,*
> *And if you will but follow me*
> *The thrilling story will be told.*

On the main deck, where the bell hangs, this one—with a round, rolling rhyme suited to the theme:

> *This is the bell*
> *That tolled so well*
> *At the battle of Trafalgar*
> *Where Nelson fell:*

He fell on deck,
He died below—
Follow me and the place I'll show.

When we came to the "last scene of all" the poet, I have always thought, excelled himself; rose to a really fine height. Many a handkerchief have I seen brought into use when these pathetic lines were recited:

Here, in the Middies' humble room,
Our Prince of Sailors last drew breath;
But Hope now smiles where once was Gloom,
And Peace has triumphed over death!

Smile on Sweet Hope! Sol, rend the clouds,
Wind of the West your requiem sing.
Blow, breezes blow! make taut our shrouds
As home our glorious Dead we bring.

Then followed the verse I have quoted first.

I wonder if that poem be still to the fore and in use?

In my day it was pretty well known in and around Portsmouth. Of course that is getting on for half a century now. Still it's wonderful how these old things survive and crop up where least expected. Somebody may have a copy of it yet, and the capturing of it would well repay the curio-hunter for his trouble.

The piece was interesting, too, in that it told how, when Nelson was at his mother's breast, the order for the building of the *Victory* was passed by My Lords of the Admiralty, showing that they were designed by Providence for each other. A historical fact; Nelson being born on September 29th, 1758, and the order for the *Victory* passed December 13th of the same year. There were other little touches besides that one, if I could only remember them.

However, we made the most of it in our day. It's a very fair sample, anyway, of the stuff we used to pour into the visitors—the Janes and Jarges from the country, or the 'Arrys and 'Arriets from London down for Bank Holiday. They were very liberal, too, these humble folks, and would swallow anything. Didn't we make them gape! And the yarns we spun for their benefit! . . . Of course the traditions of one's country must be upheld, and we *Victory* boys worked like slaves to give what we took to be the best of ours a push along.

CHAPTER 7

A Bad Shot—and the Result

One day, I think in the beginning of March, about one bell (half-past twelve) on the afternoon watch, I came up from below feeling particularly fine. The dinner—"toad-in-the-hole," with baked potatoes, etc.—had been splendid, and I had dined wisely and well. My belly was full, the sun was shining, the day—one of those sweet, unexpected days, for the season, peculiar to the English climate—was soft and balmy, the air laden with harbour scents, and not a ripple on the water. The ship looked lovely, her masts and cordage shimmering like a little grove with the sunlight on it. Her picture in silhouette lay stretched along the harbour with every detail showing as clear as in a looking-glass, and when I jumped up on the fo'c'sle and skipped about the rail my figure appeared like a little dancing toy on the glassy surface far below.

A letter, too, from a certain party in Dundee, had arrived by the morning post; as a matter of fact it was at that minute nestling under my flannel next my skin, for I hadn't a pocket about me, and the sweet words it contained were still warming me within like a little love-stove.

Altogether, my cherub was aloft and I was basking in the radiance of its smile.

I had come on deck with a piece of fat meat in my hand, and was prowling around looking for somebody to shy it at; but there was nobody about. What I brought it for I don't remember, maybe to fling to the gulls, lots of which circled round the ship at times. But they were all gone, too, that day.

The fat was growing warm in my hand—a fine, soft, flabby bit it was—and somehow I couldn't ling it away. What I wanted was a target or something to hit with it. But the deck, with the exception of the sentries, was deserted. I looked over the side to see if there were any heads sticking out of the ports, or if a waterman or bumboatman were passing. But no, nothing. So I turned and went below again.

As I was passing the galley I saw the ship's cook with all his mates around him in earnest confab over something. The cook seemed to be giving them a lecture on the day's dinner. They were all dressed in white, with white confectioners' caps; but whereas the mates had stains here and there on their jackets and aprons the cook himself was immaculate.

He was a pompous little man with a reddish, full-flowing beard, trimmed to perfection, and mustachios to match. His presence reminded you of one of his own coppers—round, shining, and capable of holding a lot.

He was laying it off to the four mates, with his right forefinger tapping the palm of his left hand, and they were all listening attentively. They were standing sideways on to me and hadn't noticed my approach.

One of the mates, a long-featured, tallow-coloured individual, with a terribly vacant expression, and his tongue hanging out, was leaning forward staring into the cook's face drinking in every word. You never saw anything so comical.

I said to myself, "Here's the very thing! Couldn't be a better mark!" I took deliberate aim and then let fly. By the sheerest stroke of bad luck, just as the meat left my hand the cook made a sudden turn right in my direction, the mate slued a little, and whether this influenced my aim or not I can't say, but it missed the squint-eyed mate and went splash into the cook's beard.

Then there was a hullabaloo! I sprang back and made for the ladder again, but not before he saw me. I knew I was nipped—knew it as well as though I felt the hand on my shoulder. And how these men ran aft to tell the corporal! By George, they didn't lose time. Before I was right on deck into the open air the Assembly sounded and up the boys came, wiping their lips and rubbing their lingers and all wondering what was the matter.

We were lined up in two rows, one on each side of the deck. Then the head bo'sun, followed by the cook, his mates, some corporals and one or two P.O.'s—an ominous procession for me—came slowly along inspecting every boy as they passed.

There was a lot of whispering round about me, but I heard nothing; *i.e.*, didn't let on. Every faculty I possessed was concentrated into one thrilling thought: "Will they spot me?"

Good gracious, what a long time they were in coming.

They stopped once or twice before other boys, and this raised the hope that maybe the cook hadn't twigged me after all; that I just imagined he had. I thought by giving my face a slight twist I might manage to put him off that way, for he didn't know me very well, but an instant's reflection on the fact that my own P.O. was among the crowd coming along warned me that he would be bound to notice it and draw attention to me. So I just set my teeth, looked straight forward and trusted to luck.

How I wished they would hurry up and get done with it. The excitement was terrific: I was quivering all over.

As they drew nearer I saw with the tail of my eye that the bo'sun's face was wrinkled with worry. He didn't seem to like his job. The cook was close beside him, with eyes gleaming like burning coals. The vacant face of the mate was just behind, and the slight glimpse I got of it had such an effect on my diaphragm that it nearly brought on the hiccup. I braced myself and looked straight in front.

"Here they are!"

The cook had the sardonic smile of a devil on him; his beard bristling and still shining with fat, and his hands working nervously at his sides. The moment he got my length, he stopped dead.

"*That's him!*"

The bo'sun edged him a little to one side. Did you fling that at the cook?" he said, nodding at him and frowning at me.

"Yes, sir."

Instantly his face cleared, his arms went up and he gave them a little wave, crying: "Oh, that's all right! That's all right! Pipe down!" Then in a lower tone: "Bring him before Mr. Farroll."

The dismissed boys came rushing from the other side (I was in the starboard watch) and flocked around to see who was the cause of the hubbub; but the corporals soon cleared them off. Charlie Caiman, with his eyes wide open and his head pushed forward, mouthed "What's up?" but, of course, I couldn't tell him anything. He hovered about— good old Charlie!—in the hope that I might drop him a signal which he would be able to interpret to my advantage, but, alas, nothing can be done in that way when you are in the grip of a naval "crusher" (ship's corporal). Aft I was bundled to go before the captain.

It was some minutes before Father put in an appearance, which time the cook employed in glaring at me as if he would have liked to give me "beardie." He was a venomous little toad, and looked it, so that the bo'sun trod hard upon his foot and brought him up. The bo'sun made believe it was an accident, but I saw he meant it.

At last Father came, calm, grave, dignified as usual, walking as slowly towards us as if he had Eternity to work in. The minute he hove in sight "cookie "made a start as if to run and pour his sorrows into him on the spot, but one of the corporals held him back whispering: "Steady on! Steady on!"

Father Farroll approached, surveyed us all with his benevolent countenance, straightened his back, worked his lips in a manner he had, and said:

"Well, what's all this?"

The words were no sooner out of his mouth than the cook, who could be restrained no longer, let fly:

"This damnable boy !" he began; but the corporal jerked him up, and Father, raising his hand, silenced him.

"Ship's corporal, please," he said.

The crusher then detailed the tragedy; dwelling on the horrible offence of throwing fat about the ship, while the cook spread out his beard, drew attention to the stains on his white drill—which I was sorry to see, I'll say that—and shifted about like, as we Scotch folk have it, "like a hen on a het girdle," glowering at me all the time as much as to say: "It's a good job for you that I haven't the punishing of you. I'd give you beans!"

"When did this happen?" Father asked when the corporal stopped.

"Just now, sir; not ten minutes ago. I was standing in the galley . . ." broke in the cook, when Father silenced him again.

"Quite so," he said. . . . "And how," turning to the corporal, "do you know this is the boy that did it?"

Here the bo'sun chimed up, "Oh, he confessed it himself, sir."

"Urn," said Father, stroking his chin and looking sadly at me.

"I was just telling the mates—" began the cook again, when Father turned sharply upon him:

"Cook!" he said, with some asperity, "be good enough to speak when you are spoken to. . . . Did—er . . . had you any trouble," he resumed, addressing the bo'sun in his usual placid, precise way of talking—"I mean had you any bother with this boy before you got him to make the confession? "

"No, sir," the bo'sun answered heartily. "None whatever, none in the least. He owned up right away when the question was put to him."

"Urn," murmured Father again, nodding his head, "Urn!"

Then his eyes rested full upon me—and, oh dear! didn't I feel a pitiable object under their scrutiny. They were soft, brown eyes, calm as summer lakes—just like the eyes of a dog I once had—they fell upon you like a benediction. I felt I deserved hanging for bringing such a pained look into them.

He regarded me for about half a minute and then set his head a-shaking—"Teh, tch, tch! he said. "Boy, boy! what sort of conduct is this? . . . Are you aware of what deck you are standing upon? . . . Do you not know that the great Nelson, the saviour of his country, trod these boards? That this ship, the *Victory*—is the most sacred piece of timber that floats? . . . Do you not realize that? . . . Are you aware"—a terrible sternness coming into his tone—"that such actions as you have been guilty of bring discredit upon an illustrious name, tarnish a beautiful tradition, and violate the sanctity of this glorious fabric"—taking in the whole ship with a wave of his hand. . . . "Are you not ashamed of yourself? . . . Look at the cook"—I was afraid to look at him for the venom in his eyes scorched me—"Look at his fine, white clothes . . . and his beard—" here the cook's lips curled into a snarl—"all smeared and smudged with that oily stuff. . . . This is bad! . . . How could you do it? . . . I wonder what Nelson would say to this? . . .

"You know"—he paused for a little, worked his lips, and then continued—"You know, Nelson was once a boy just like yourself. But he was a good boy, . . . a brave boy . . . a fearless boy . . . a-a-a- yes, I should say a mischievous boy, too, in a way. But not this sort of way. . . . Oh, no! This isn't mischievous; it is—a—diabolical!" Here the cook glared at me in such a way that he drew my head round in his direction in spite of myself. It was as though I were mesmerised—and the look of him was so ferocious, and the vacant face of the mate behind him so lugubrious, that I nearly had another fit of the hiccup. Honestly, it was a rotten time altogether.

"No," Father went on; "this isn't what Nelson would have done. Nor is it what Nelson would have liked any of *his boys* to do. No, no!"

Another pause, while he seemed lost in thought, and worked his lips, sometimes pursing them in the way you do when you are going to kiss somebody.

"Now," he resumed again, "you seem to have the makings of a

good boy in yourself. The way you owned up to your fault proves this, and I've great hope for you. . . . The way I shall punish you is this: You will stand in front of Nelson's picture to-night for two hours. You will think about him, meditate upon him, take him into you, as it were— *absorb* him—let him permeate your whole being! This you will do ... for two hours—five to seven—this evening . . . and let it be a lesson to you. . . . Now, remember "wagging his finger. . . . "Well, that's all, pipe down!"

He clasped his hands behind his back again, and walked away.

The cook looked murder, but he daren't do anything. "Two hours first watch!" he growled; "My God! why, I would have given him ten years in Lewis!" (Lewis is the naval prison).

The corporal said: "'Tion! Five to seven at the half deck. Right turn—dismiss!"

In one minute I was on the fo'c'sle, with Charlie and a crowd of the other fellows around me, telling them all about it. They laughed over the story and warmly congratulated me, saying that Father must have been in a particularly good mood to let me off so easily. I thought so myself, blessing my stars. But I thought, too, that the chance I gave him of enlarging upon his hero—who was mine also—I wonder if he sensed that?—did more for me than anything.

CHAPTER 8

Absorbing Nelson

Promptly on the stroke of the bell I landed on the half-deck, and there was the corporal waiting for me.

It was Big Moss, the singer. He frowned heavily as he put me in front of the picture, and then, sticking out his lower jaw, said:

"Now, you stand there as if you was made o' marble, and no shinanigin. Just let me catch you with your eyes off Lord Nelson's face for one half-second of time during the next two hours, and"—he nodded three or four times with deep omen—"you'll see what happens! . . . I'm a-watching of you—don't you forget that!" With which comforting assurance he went off, leaving me to my vigil.

As I have said, it had been a fine day, and now night began to fall in heavenly beauty. At that moment a lovely sunset was filling the western sky—the harbour, the land behind, the town, the ships, the millionaire's yacht in the creek—everything bathed in glorious light. When I left the deck the two forts at Spithead were shining like jewels. Even Gosport looked pretty; while the grimy coal hulks—saucy old warships they were in their day!—took on some of their former grandeur and lay along the shore like a string of black pearls right up to Whale Island, where the *Vernon* and *Asia* lay twinkling like twin stars.

I was loath to leave it all. The rest of the boys were now enjoying the scene to their heart's content, while here was I compelled to stare at a faded old thing of a picture and forgo a pleasure my soul loved.

I cursed that cook; cursed my luck; cursed everybody and everything! . . . Why didn't I take a surer aim? . . . Why did I let him see me? . . . What the mischief made that vacant-faced idiot move just at the wrong moment? . . . And the cook, too! . . . Why didn't I duck before he had time to spot me? ... I was a fool! . . . The shot went home anyway . . . But now; look at this—this took the gilt off the gingerbread properly.

The little pock-puddin'! He had seen me once during the afternoon and shaken his fist at me, crying: —"By God, don't let me get hold of you!" But—ach-him! He couldn't run for nuts. Just waddled like a duck. I could jump over his head. . . . Just wait! I would pay him out for this.

So ran my thoughts. That I had only myself to blame; that to smear a man with grease, and that man the one by whose skill I had been furnished with an excellent dinner, was a very silly and rotten thing to do. That, moreover, I had got off pretty lightly and should be jolly thankful—these and other considerations never gave me the least bother. I was wild at being "kept in," hearing my shipmates chirping and skipping about on deck like wild woodlarks and myself missing the fun. Blast that cook There was a scrape as of a foot somewhere near; but I hadn't spoken nor moved my head, so I was all right.

I looked at the face in the frame. The light was dim and the features not very distinct. But it was a sweet face, wistful, calm and benign. The look of it soothed me. The expression was lamb-like—not bold and heroic as you would have expected such a redoubtable naval leader's to be. And yet there was something about the face that hinted of these qualities, too. But its strong point was gentleness.

I whispered—very, very low to it—"You seem to sympathise with me. . . . Good old Nelson! . . . Were you ever in a corner like this? . . . Pretty rotten, isn't it?" as a wild yell from on deck caused me to crunch my teeth.

But another stealthy movement nearby told me to watch myself, so I stared at that picture for all I was worth, "absorbing" it, letting it "into me," "permeate my whole being," as Father had commanded me to, and thought about Nelson till my brain reeled.

This went on for half an hour or so, then it began to be monotonous. Gazing fixedly at anything for a length of time does get a bit trying, especially if the light is dim and the object you are looking at dimmer even than the light.

Besides, this picture of Nelson, though an object to be revered and cherished, was hardly the thing for a boy to find interest in, in the waning light of a March evening. It was faded, wrinkled, criss-crossed with a hundred lines from top to bottom like the face of an old, old man. Nevertheless I loved it, loved to look at it, came often voluntarily to look at it—in my spare time!

But to be compelled—and here I thought that Father had missed the mark as completely as I myself had done when I threw the meat at the cook's mate—to be compelled to stand and stare at it now, on such a lovely evening, took away all the reverence I had for my hero and made me loathe him.

I couldn't see him—didn't want to see him! What I wanted was to be on deck enjoying the sunset and sharing the larks. . . . I groaned in spirit.

Sometimes when a louder shout than usual came down telling of some extra joyous freak of play, I grit my teeth and felt I would like to take the picture down, jump into the water, swim ashore, and bury it in some marshy hole round about Gosport.

But I daren't move—daren't look round, for if I did Corporal Moss would have me as sure as fate.

By and by, when I had been staring about an hour, I began to get dizzy and the picture to take funny shapes. Sometimes I thought the face lengthened and frowned at me; then, while I looked, the upper lip would slowly and visibly get longer, the lower one drop and the mouth open as if it were going to bite. Sometimes the face grew round and grinned. Sometimes it seemed that the tongue shot out and the whole face jeered at me.

Sometimes the head seemed to stand out from the canvas, so that I could see all round it, and become so clear and distinct, the eye glowing, and such a noble expression on the features, that I fancied it was Nelson in real life I was looking at. Then it would become smaller and gradually fade away before my eyes till it went out of sight altogether.

Sometimes I seemed to see right through it—through the bulkhead—through the ship—through everything, in fact—away beyond Whale Island.

It was terrifying!

Once, very, very cautiously, I took a look around. Not a soul was in sight! I had the whole big deck to myself. The corporal was evidently sure of me! I took a wide, luxurious survey—at the beams overhead, the ladders, the ship's furniture, through the entry-port at the country, gradually dimming in the twilight, and then back to Nelson again, feeling refreshed.

I thought to myself: "These fellows"—meaning my chattering shipmates on deck—couldn't I hear them—"These fellows think that this is a light punishment. I hope some of them may get it—they'll see! . . ."

Then I began to think of what Father Farroll had said about Nelson. . . . I took another cautious look around—Nobody about! . . . The corporal was gone! . . . away! . . . He had got tired! . . . I wished he would begin to sing; then I would be sure of him; but second thoughts told me he couldn't do that, as he was on watch. Anyway, he was gone . . . After all, I hadn't much longer to do now . . .

I swept the deck, glancing right and left, up and down, feeling quite joco now, and then back to Nelson again.

"Ah," I whispered, "you were a nice boy . . . a *v-e-r-y* nice boy! . . . a brave boy . . . a fearless boy . . . ' a-a- (mimicking Father) yes—a mischievous boy!' . . . but not a boy like me. . . . Oh, no! . . . You were a good boy! . . . I'm a bad boy!—Yah-h-h!" Nelson's eyes seemed wide open, "standing in his head," as the saying is. I lifted my right hand, put the thumb to my nose, spread out the fingers till the little one landed right on the tip of the immortal nose of Nelson, and was luxuriating in the glow that comes upon achievement to the Greatly Daring when—

"MY GOD!"

came in an awed whisper behind me.

It was the corporal, and he had caught me!

Shall I ever forget the next five minutes? . . . Never in this world!

The corporal rushed at me, crying:

"You devil! You gallows hound!" He got me by the shoulder, whirled me round as if I had been a "peerie," shook me till I actually felt the bones in my skull rattle together, pushed me towards the picture, and I had a wild thought that he was going to put my head through it, but he changed his mind, swept me over to the ship's side, and dashed me bodily against it.

Then down he plumped on to a little form nearby, jerked me across his knee and oh, dear, dear! The memory of this experience is almost as painful as the reality. At every slap, breathing hard the while like a man in a wrestling bout, he muttered: "You—little—devil! You would do—that to the—Admiral. Thought—I wasn't—looking—eh? But I was—I caught you—fine—didn't I? What—the devil—d'ye mean—by it?"

I was limp and listless. The breath was all knocked out of my body. I couldn't speak—couldn't wriggle even. Just lay like a log and let him do what he liked with me. . . . He pushed me off his leg, but before

53

I reached the deck he had me up on my feet again, and glaring into my face, hissed:

"You born devil! You vile varmint! . . . I won't report you, for if I did Mr. Farroll would go mad. But I—I—I—damn—I'll flay you alive! What d'ye mean by it? . . ."

The standing on my feet, and this little respite from jostling, though short, was long enough to let me get my breath back; and the news I wasn't to be reported put new life into me.

"Oh, sir!" I wailed, clasping my hands and looking at him imploringly—"please don't hit me anymore. I didn't mean anything. I didn't really. It was only a joke. Nelson's my hero! I love him!"

This seemed only to infuriate the corporal more than ever. He gripped me in such a fierce embrace that he nearly made me pigeon-breasted, lifted and bumped me down till I bit my tongue, and just about swallowed part of it. But even while he did so I felt that Corporal Moss was a good fellow, for he kept his voice low, so as not to bring the others on the scene and give me away.

"So that's it, is it?—you little mischievous monkey! . . . Nelson's your hero, is he? . . . And you love him, do you? . . . And that's the way you show your love, is it? . . . And it was all a joke was it? . . . You little imp! . . . Damn your eyes. I'll teach you to joke with your betters! . . . Ur-r-r-r! . . ."

At every pause he gave me a shake, and at the last such a terrific one that I thought I should fall to pieces. "Will you ever do that again?" he enquired vehemently, with his eyes bursting out of his head.

"No! never sir! Never!" I panted. "Never again, sir; believe me!"

"Down on your knees and beg Lord Nelson's pardon! "

Down I flopped in front of the picture, and raising my hands in the attitude of prayer, cried:

"Oh! dear Lord Nelson, forgive me! I beg your pardon! I'm sorry. I'm very sorry! I am—I really am Corporal Moss," I cried, turning swiftly round and appealing to the petty officer, then back again to the picture—"Forgive me, sir! I'll never do it again—never!"

I could have sworn when I turned so sharply that I had seen a grin on the corporal's face, but when I looked again at the end of my supplication it was as grim as ever.

"Get up," he commanded.

I put my hands on the deck and hoisted myself up as though I were half dead; but, in reality, not so very much the worse, all said and done.

Perhaps he knew I was shamming, for he took hold of my serge and jerked me on to my feet. Then he shook his big fist in my face and said:

"Now, look here"—his chin was out as far as it would go—"you thank your lucky stars it wasn't another man got you, for if it had been, he would have peeled the skin off you and reported you as well. Will you stop these monkey tricks?"

"Yes, sir; oh yes!"

"Then get out!" and with that he lifted me with the side of his boot a good six feet along the gangway; and I was up the ladder and into the fresh air before his foot got back to the deck again—I'm very sure I was.

I ran on to the fo'c'sle, jumped the rail, and snuggled into the knightheads just under the lee of the figurehead. What fine places those dear old ships had for a boy to hide in. There I sat for an hour, rubbing myself gently and enjoying the beauty of the evening till it was time to turn in. During the remainder of my stay in the *Victory*, I need not say that I kept well out of sight of Father Farroll and Corporal Moss—ay, and the cook, too!

CHAPTER 9

H.M.S. Swallow

About a week after this, Charlie Caiman got orders to pack his bag for the *Black Prince*, and I to do the same for the *Duke of Wellington*, so we had to part brass rags, poor Charlie and I, and say "goodbye."

This we did with some feeling, for we had been good chums. I never saw him again, nor heard of or from him; nor yet of Corporal Moss or Father Farroll or any of the others.

That is always the way in the Navy. You meet a man on this ship or that, get chummy with him, spend a little time together, bid him "so-long" at the end of it and—there you are. You never behold each other again.

However, it's all in the day's work and you get accustomed to it.

The *Duke* at this time was the Guardship at Portsmouth. I was only a few days aboard of her.

One day when working on the poop I heard a signalman call to his mate: "Hey, Bill; look at that little craft. Ain't she a beauty?" I looked, too, and saw the prettiest little ship my eyes had ever rested on.

She was painted black with a white streak at her deck line, and a row of twinkling scuttles fore and aft, barring right amidships. Her copper shone like a band of gold, and glittered in the water like a halo around her. She was *barque* rigged, with her sails lying like a coating of snow along her yards, and had just left the dockyard. She reminded me of a little girl newly dressed for her first day at school. A prettier picture you never saw. A sweet little funnel with a black top on it peeping just above the netting showed that she was also fitted with steam.

Four boats swung from her davits, two abreast of the funnel, and two abaft the mainmast. The black muzzle of a new 7-inch gun frowned from the only porthole which broke the line of her bulwarks; and her gangway ladder, which was lipping the water, was composed of eight steps. I drank in all her details greedily, saying to myself: "You're a bonnie wee thing. I wish I were going to you."

Little did I think that I was destined to spend four of the happiest years of my life in her, and pay off from her with a storehouse of memories that I wouldn't exchange even now for the worth of the British Islands But so it proved. It was H.M.S. *Swallow* I was looking at. In three days I was aboard of her, and within a week outward bound for the West Coast of Africa.

H.M.S. *SWALLOW*

1st Class Gunboat. Displacement 805 tons. Dimensions: 170'x29'x10'. H.P. 11.1 knots. Twin Screws. Guns: 1-7", 6½ ton rifled M.L., 2-40 rifled B.L. Built 1869.

CHAPTER 10

Outward Bound

My recollections of the *Swallow*, however, begin with our first evening at sea. We had been played out of Portsmouth Harbour by the band of the *St. Vincent*, got a fine send-off in the shape of three rousing cheers from the *Duke*, and had steamed past the Blockhouse and forts in great spirits.

In the afternoon sail had been set, and the little vessel in her new, milk-white canvas must have looked a pretty picture to the smacks and schooners and other craft we passed on the way. Inboard she looked just as pretty. Her decks stretched from fo'c'sle-head to taffrail like ruled paper the colour of ivory. A sweet little capstan, painted white, stood close abaft the fore companion—a structure for all the world like a prompter's box in a theatre, and the two together formed the daintiest set-off to a ship's deck you could imagine. Her engine-room hatches were open, and the glass of these, and the binnacles, and the wheel and the cabin windows on the poop shot the sun back in flashes with every movement of her. Everything about her was new, trig and fresh.

The capstan had a drumhead of brass which was polished to such a degree of brightness that it seemed to attract most of the rays to itself and then send them scattering in all directions like fiery lances. The companion was brown, had a sliding top, and was polished too, so that you saw your face in it almost as clearly as you do in a mirror. This was the entrance to the lower deck, the men's living room, an apartment extending from well abaft the foremast right into the eyes of the ship—a roomy space, bright and airy and clean as bone. It contained six big messes: four for bluejackets, one for marines, and one for stokers, with a smaller one abaft the ladder for the first class P.O.'s.

A row of lockers for holding clothes, each about eighteen inches long and the height of your knee, ran along the ship's side into the fore-peak, under the mess racks, with the tables placed fore and aft in front of them. The tables could be triced up when not in use.

Farther aft there were cabins to port and starboard for the bo'sun, and the chief gunner's mate; a little bunk of an office for the ship's corporal, who was also acting "Jaundy"; the steward's pantry, etc. These with the gunner's chest (a huge piece of furniture which was lashed to two stanchions amidships, and was big enough to allow two men to enjoy a snooze on top of it, in a watch below), the drinking water tank, and, of course, the ordinary mess gear-crockery, tin dishes, kettles and all the rest of it, completed the housing arrangements. A hatchway abaft the P.O.'s mess led to the tank room where the fresh water supply was stored.

Altogether the lower deck of the *Swallow* was as tidy and cheerful a sea parlour as you would have found afloat; and when we all got into it, at a meal hour, say, or when both watches were off in harbour (especially on Saturdays, which was "scrub and wash mess-deck" day), and we started to sing—then we made the rafters ring. There were seventy odd common Jacks in that choir, and everyone did his little bit, or tried to.

Sometimes an argument would crop up, bringing twenty or thirty into it all trumpeting their opinions at the same time. Talk about a shindy It was like W. S. Gilbert's politicians in the street, or Burns's scene in the pub at the "Holy Fair." Boys weren't allowed to take part in these debates. The tradition was that nobody could argue or sit on the mess-table till he could show hair on his breast.

Sometimes a quarrel took place, and then you would hear a few pithy sentences, fairly well flavoured with salt, regarding one or other of the contestant's fathers or mothers or grandmothers. (Isn't it queer how men always drag the ancestors of an opponent into the argument and sneer them out of all shape and form?) It was amusing to listen to them. If the dispute took a bitter turn the other fellows usually slipped quietly on deck, if the weather was fine, and left the two to worry the bit out between them; if it were foul, then they rose in a body, put the foot down and stopped it.

Sometimes there was a real fight: a regular downright bout of fisti-cuffs. This was usually settled on the fo'c'sle, and the captain winked at it, believing that the men would be better friends when it was over.

And he was right. I don't remember any of these scraps leaving bad feeling behind them.

But this did not happen often. We were a happy crowd as a rule, and rather fond of one another. Really, I don't recall much unpleasantness on that little ship.

And after all, it is only the pleasant things in life that ought to be remembered. There is enough dirt about without storing it up. That's my philosophy.

Looking back, though, and wishing to tell the real truth, I believe I myself was the cause of a good many shindies that might have been avoided had circumstances been different.

You see, I was the only *known* Scotchman in the ship. Certainly there were others, two, but they weren't much good to me, and I didn't get hold of that fact till the ship had been over two years in commission. They were old hands, and, knowing that they were very much in the minority, had the sense to keep their mouths shut regarding nationality.

One was a P.O. named Milne, hailing from Musselburgh, the other a marine, Hughie McGhee, who died only last year at Kilwinning. He was keeper of a railway crossing there, and was in my house a week or two before "The Boatman" called. I had hopes that Hughie would live to see this book out, for he was keenly interested in it, but—ah, well!

So these two didn't count. They moved in a different orbit to mine, and though the ship was small we seldom came in contact.

There were also three Welshmen—"Old Taff," a stoker (I don't know what his real name was. I question if he knew it himself, for that was the only title he was ever known by in the Service, and he had been a long time in it), Muddy Jones was the second of the Welshies, and Shortie Edwards, a rare dancer, the third.

Then we had four sprigs from the green hills of Erin—Mick Carne, a long, ungainly chap, who was always deserted; Mick Leonard, who couldn't be beaten at telling weird Banshee stories, or reading your fortune from your teacup; Cussack, a wild boy this when the drink was in him; and little Tommy Logan, as genial a wee chap as ever you met. All the others were English. Nice fellows they were, but some of them used to "rag" me terribly about Scotland, saying that the people there were uncivilised—bare-legged savages who lived on oats and couldn't do anything but brew whisky—and so on. They also called me "Old Burgoo," "Oatmeal face," and other pet names.

I wasn't long from school then, and being fairly well up in history, the things they said about Scotland put my back up. I would retaliate by saying that Englishmen should thank God that Scotland was so near them. That without her help they wouldn't have got out of some of the nasty corners their own foolishness had led them into quite so easily as they did, mentioning Lucknow, Sir John Moore, Cochrane, Duncan of Camperdown, and others.

"Who started the great Bank of England you all brag so much about?" I would shout at them. "Who gave you steam to send your ships along and make sailors' work easier? . . . Who started your Navy first of all, if it comes to that?"

"Not a burgoo-eatin' Scotchman anyway!" they would shout back.

"Was it no'?" I would yell, "you just look and see!"

Sometimes, just to rile them, I would trot out Bannockburn, and then, of course, there was blood for supper!

So I needn't tell you that I had a fight nearly every day. First with Tom, then with Dick, then with Harry. But it was always *me* who figured in these fracas. Billy, the first lieutenant, used to give it to me hot for coming before him so often.

The upshot of it all was that I won for myself a name for being quarrelsome, and was called a disturber of the ship's peace right at the start of the commission. Many a lecture and weary punishment I had to suffer, which might easily have been missed had I shown a little more commonsense. But I learnt in time, I'm glad to say!

CHAPTER 11

At Sea

I belonged to the afterpart of the ship—a main topman—but I wasn't allowed to go aloft as yet; a provision for which I was devoutly thankful—for while it was all very well to caper about among the spars and rigging of the training ships, which stood as firm as churches, it was different here. Even the slight roll made climbing into these airy heights a fearsome business. So I blessed the skipper when I heard him pass the order prohibiting the boys from mounting the rigging till they had found their sea legs.

Chancing to glance forward, I saw a sight that warmed my heart to the core and sent my thoughts homeward with a bound. It was a large oblong stamp on the fore-topsail:

This was the name of the firm which had wrought and supplied the canvas, and the look of it brought back a thousand memories. I knew the mill. I knew the whole district. Every stone in it was as familiar to me as the fingers on my hand. Indeed, my mother was working in that mill at that very moment. Poor wee mother! She would be lonely now. The tears started to my eyes and blurred the topsail. But I rubbed them away with my cap, whispering "Cheer up I we'll have that rose-covered house yet, and then she'll be happy," and went about my work hugging myself.

By this time we were well out to sea. It was pleasant to feel the heave of the vessel under your foot, and the sensation, now that the engines were stopped, of swishing over the water with no sound about you but the wind aloft and the rush of the bow-wave.

We were heading for Queenstown, our first stopping- place. It was the twentieth of May, 1877. A lovely day it had been, a fine fresh breeze blowing, and the sky so clear, and the sea so gentle-looking and sweet that I thought nothing on earth could compare with the life of a sailor.

Among my messmates was a boy about my own age, nicknamed "Spooney." This had been given him on account of his having been seen sitting on Southsea Common along with a nice, buxom little girl, and holding her hand, some days previously.

During the afternoon, while we were at work restowing the fore, hold, Spooney had been unmercifully badgered about this business, and there had been a row at tea-time through a boy in number one mess piping over to him in a shrill voice:

"Spooney, dear; is it nice to be kissed by a young female?" Spooney had set upon him and nearly swallowed him whole. He hated the name; but he was going to change it soon, although he didn't know that then.

Now it was the first dog-watch, from four to six. There were only a few cases of sugar to restow, some bags of biscuits and a cask or two, and these the watch on deck were to look after. The rest of us were sitting or standing about looking at the land, which lay all aboard on the starboard side but getting dimmer and dimmer every minute. In little groups, some standing on the coamings of the hatchways, some on the fore-bits, some on the fo'c'sle, the men were gathered in the forepart of the ship, the officers much the same way aft, gazing over the starboard side:

Upon the fast receding hills that dim
and distant rise.

Not a word was spoken. Everyone was busy with his own thoughts, picturing, perhaps, the last scene with a loving mother, wife or sweet-heart. I was sitting on top of the capstan, and there was a cask of treacle with the lid half off in front of me. I stuck in my finger and took a lick before climbing up. Spooney was perched on some boxes below me, his head just low enough for me to see nicely over, and we had the cask between us, its flavour rising to my nostrils and reminding me of the balmy days of the *St. Vincent* and the nightly dole of "scoff and basher,"

Suddenly an ordinary seaman, called Lucks, who was a bit of a musician, struck a chord on his concertina and began to play, of all tunes, the one most suitable to the scene and the hour, "Isle of Beauty, fare thee well." He had not got beyond the second or third bar when Curly Millet, another O.D., a tall, slim fellow, hailing from Canterbury, joined in with the song. There was no premeditation or thought of effect in either of their heads. It was a purely spontaneous overflow, and expressed exactly what was in everybody's heart at the minute. Indeed, the incident seemed so natural that we were not even surprised at it. Rapt in attention we listened, while Curly, in a clear, quivering voice, sang the pathetic words of England's sweetest lyric, Lucks playing the while as if his whole soul were in the melody:

'Tis the hour when happy faces
Gather round the taper's light,
Who will fill our vacant places?
Who will sing our songs tonight?

What would I not give to wander
Where my old companions dwell!
Absence makes the heart grow fonder,
Isle of beauty, fare thee well!

It was a lovely evening. Regular "ladies' weather." With the passing of the sun the wind had fallen and the sky turned like maple, dappled all over with beautiful spots like the eyes of angels looking down upon us, and the sea stretched away, a broad belt of azure slashed here and there with silver. A gentle breeze a little abaft the beam blew us along, and there was nothing to disturb the performers. The only sounds heard were the lap-lap of the wavelets licking the side of the ship as they flowed by, the flap of a restless sail, or creak of a mast, and these seemed to form the ideal orchestra necessary to complete the accompaniment. They went through the song to the end, and oh, it was sweet—sweet!

Not an officer or man lost a word or note of the music. Surely never was anything so appropriate. There, before us, lay the land, the "Isle of Beauty," perhaps the very scene that inspired the poet to write his song, with all its tender associations and memories. The shades of evening were closing around, and would soon hide it from our view.

Perhaps we might see it again, perhaps never—who could tell?

For a minute or two after the song was ended a wistful yearning sadness fell upon the ship. The silence became even deeper and the strain on the heart-strings tenser. A mist rose up before my eyes that dimmed and blurred them, but I dared not move to rub it away. We seemed to be all under a spell, which nobody cared to be the first to break. How it would have been broken I have no idea if Providence had not taken a hand.

We were straining to get as much of the old country as possible before it would be blotted out, when a sound as of something being sucked into a vortex was heard. It was close to me, and I looked down and saw a pair of boots staring up at me from the cask of treacle. Instinctively I made a grab at them, and, with a cry of astonishment, followed by a wild yell of laughter, all the men were round the spot in a minute. The combined efforts of two or three soon cleared the Owner of the boots from his glutinous bath and revealed poor Spooney—but what a sight! I fell off the capstan, laughing, and almost broke my head against the coamings of the fore-hatch. The treacle was pretty thick and stuck to him like glue, and he had to be hung over the barrel for some time till they got it partly squeegeed off him.

I think I see him yet trying to open his mouth to get breath. He couldn't do it, and one of the men noticing his distress, clawed the stuff away and gave him free passage. Then it opened like the maw of a cod-fish and sucked in everything around it. When he was half cleaned they carried him aft and played the hot-water hose on him, but it was some time before he got his eyes properly open. What a laugh it was! I don't think I ever had one like it in all my life. Coming as it did, too, it was a veritable godsend, although the revulsion of feeling was so strong that I had a catch in my throat for hours afterwards every time I drew a long breath. Spooney told me that night when we were turning in that the song had had such an effect on him, that he fancied himself sitting in the armchair at home, and was leaning back to enjoy it thoroughly when he capsized into the treacle.

However, he was none the worse for his dip. Rather better, for the nickname of "Spooney," which he detested, was dropped, and "Molasses" substituted, and he didn't care a rap for that. It did us all good, too, for it gave us something in common to talk about and laugh over, and in that way drew us together.

And that treacle was relished, every drop of it, with devil a bit of its flavour impaired!

During the night a storm came on which nearly blew us out of the water, and turned all my ideas of a sailor's life upside down. If you want to see quick—and spiteful—changes of weather, try the English Channel. I thought the end of the world had come. I was so sea-sick that I wished myself dead a thousand times and remembered no more till the ship was lying anchored at Queenstown.

One of the men, old Neddy Pearce, bless him!—the oldest man aboard, older even than the skipper, and yet only an A.B. on account of his love for the grog-tub—brought me a basin of tea the flavour of which was so delicious, and I so cold, that I gulped it down right away. But it was made with salt water, and brought on such a fit of retching that I thought my boots would come up. It did me good, however, for after that I never experienced sea-sickness again.

And now I always advise anybody who is likely to suffer the awful tortures of *mal de mer* to try that cure. Make a cup of tea with sea water and you'll find it works wonders. You are "*cured with a hair of the dog that bit you*," as the saying is.

CHAPTER 12

Making for Madeira

When I "came to" at Queenstown, and Neddy's tea had done its good work, the world looked sweet again and I felt hungry enough to eat a Mohammedan.

By this time the ship was full of Irish people all busy trying to sell trinkets of one kind or another—beaded slippers, dainty little hand-made handkerchiefs, fancy mats, and lots of other things.

When I got to the mess I found an old woman sitting on my locker contentedly eating my dinner, which Spooney—or, rather, Molasses now—had kept for me, but some of the others must have given to her.

I said to her, with my whole soul in my eyes and voice, "Mother; that's my dinner you're eating!"

"Is it, now, me son," she said, in a fine rich brogue; "sure, thin, an' its splendid."

"Ah, but," said I, watching her put a big hunk of beef into her mouth, "I'm hungry. I haven't had any grub for the last two days."

She looked at me with her big, broad face full of sympathy, and her mouth full of meat, munching the while with great relish, and waited till she had got it swallowed. Then she said:

"Think o' that now, me poor *bouchal*."

"Ah, well; you're sure of your dinner tomorrow, an' that's more than I can say," and in went another piece.

I hadn't the heart to quarrel with her, so I went on deck again and under the fo'c'sle, where I had a "guid greet" to myself, for I was terribly hungry. Morris, the captain's cook's-mate saw me and came over and asked what was the matter.

I told him with many sobs and gulps.

"Is that all?" he said. "Cheer up!" He brought me a huge plateful of scraps from the cabin and wardroom—beef, potatoes, pie-crust, chicken-legs, which I polished off and then licked the plate clean, thanking the old woman for putting me in the way of such a feast.

We stayed two days at Queenstown. I wrote home to my mother and the girl telling them all about it, and describing the lovely scene of the hill slopes above the town, which were divided up into little squares, all in various stages of cultivation and, viewed from where we were lying, looked like a draught-board. The hills form a semi-circle round the bay, with Cork and the Great Island on the right, Spike Island, a big fort (prison, I think, in my time), on the left, and the town between.

I never saw such green anywhere. It seemed to shine and stand out by itself. The weather was delicious, and the bay, lying pure and clean as crystal with the hills and the town mirrored in it, made a picture that I have never forgotten.

We were now under weigh for Madeira. As we steamed down the Lough I felt as fit as a fiddle, and when the ship got into the open and began to tumble about, never a qualm had I. I had found my sea legs, too, and could adapt myself to the motion as well as though my mother had been a sailor and I born on the rolling billow. And it was all needed; for here life was different altogether from what it had been in the training-ship. There, you were molly-coddled—wrapped in cotton wool so to speak. Here, life was bare and no humbug about it: you had your bit to do and were expected to do it and look pleasant. There, it was mostly make-believe. Here, life was calling in earnest, and it was up to you to answer promptly and toe the line like a man.

In the training-ship you had been grounded in all the arts (and graces) that go to the make-up of that wonderful soul, The Handy Man (and he is a wonderful soul, mind you, a proper Stick-at-Nothing!) You were tailor, laundry-maid, kitchen-wench, carpenter or cook, just as occasion needed. Your mind was also drilled. You were taught reverence for good things, self-respect, self-reliance, deference to those better than yourself—everything in fact but servility. Nothing of that in the Navy! You were taught seamanship, gunnery, boat-pulling, mast-climbing, gymnastics, and everything necessary for keeping the body fit and the mind clean. What you had to do now was turn these little bits of instruction to good account and learn more.

The food, too, was different. Not nearly so plentiful or palatable as in *Mama*, as the training-ship was called. Strict Navy allowance— pound and pint, and no more. Pound of biscuits (hard tack), stowed in bags (for the biscuit-tin wasn't invented then), and usually full of wee-vils. These are small brown insects, like bugs—smelling like them, too, by Jove!—and very much alive. I've actually seen a man lay down a piece of biscuit to explain a point to a mate with whom he was argu-ing, and when he turned to take up the biscuit again it had wandered to another part of the table! Then you had your pound of beef ("salt 'oss"), or pork, usually with pea soup that you could see through, or "Fanny Adams" (soup and *bouilli*) with preserved potatoes, on alternate days. A little flour was occasionally served out for making doughboys, and some raisins and currants for a plum duff on a Sunday. That, with a pint of cocoa for breakfast, and one of tea in the afternoon, with your drink of lime-juice at six bells in the afternoon watch, was your daily ration. Of course, you could always buy from the canteen, but the pay didn't allow of going to any great length in that direction.

At eighteen you were rated Ordinary Seaman, and allowed your glass of grog at dinner-time. This stuff I never could be bothered with. But I "took mine up" to save trouble. There weren't many teetotallers about in those days and they lived in bad odour on the lower deck. It needed the influence of a Miss Agnes Weston and a few more of her stamp to bring common-sense into the Navy.

There was a deal of drunkenness in my time, although the habit was beginning to "go out of fashion." A man would return to the ship after a four-days' leave and hail his chum with:

"Say, Bill. Wot a 'oliday!—drunk all the time! Never saw Ole Ja-maicar (the sun) once!"

And his mate would reply, smacking his lips:

"Prime! My turn's coming!"

It was a great nuisance forward, and must have been a sore trial aft; for I must say, to the credit of the officers, they tried both by example and precept to bring about a better state of things. But it had its laugh-able side, too.

One of my messmates was a little man named Josie Deakin. Josie drank like a haddock. He could never get enough. He was the owner of a pair of whiskers which were the delight of the girls wherever we touched. They were of a lovely auburn hue. Josie was vastly proud of them. He went ashore one night at St. Paul de Loanda, on the West Coast of Africa, and was brought back so "absolutely fu'" that he had to be hoisted aboard with a watch-tackle. They flung him down on the deck and left him there, snoring like a hog. During the night somebody came along and shaved off the right side of his moustache and his left whisker, leaving his face like a draughtboard. Then the mosquitoes which swarm in that quarter of the globe fell upon him and made a night of it. When he awoke in the morning his face was a sight for the gods, and almost killed the ship's company. The parts shorn of the hair and his brow and nose were swollen as large as turnips, and he had a bump under his chin like a pouter pigeon. His hands were like freak potatoes. His eyes were nowhere—you couldn't see them. Anyone who knows the West Coast will tell you what mosquitoes can do. You never saw such a sight in all your life. Laugh! Oh, dear! I laugh yet when I think about it.

Of course he had to shave clean; but that only made matters worse, by turning his face into a thing like a survey map with the hills and hollows all marked. When we fell in for inspection the captain, followed by the first lieutenant—who is called Billy, or No. 1—passed slowly down the line till he came to Josie, when he gave a violent start which nearly shook his cap off. He glared at him for about a minute, and then blurted out:

"Who is this man?" turning to No. 1.

Billy, who wore a monocle, screwed the glass into his eye, and peered at Josie.

"Man, who are you ?" he shouted. "Don't you hear the captain?"

"Deakin, sir."

"Deakin!" snapped the skipper, staring at him. "Good heavens! What have you done to your face? Where's your whiskers? Get them on at once!" and down the line he went. The situation was too trying for him. Josie, poor soul, had to toe the line, and got fourteen days 10A for that caper. But it didn't abate his thirst all the same.

This is a little before my story, but let it stand.

CHAPTER 13

Parading the West Coast

We were hardly out of our own latitude when a gale sprang up which blew us into the Bay of Biscay and kept our heels dancing to the tune of "In t' gallant sails!" "Hands reef topsails!" "Hands set fore-and-aft sails!" Hands here, hands there, hands everywhere and all the time from morning to night, and all through the night, too, while it lasted; the wind blowing the breath out of your body or lifting you off the foot-ropes, and you clinging to whatever you were at with one hand while working away with the other. That experience (for I was now going aloft and doing my share with the others, and was a top-gallant yard man) taught me the art of taking a grip and keeping it that has proved very useful to me since, situated as I am and liable to fall at any moment. Then the weather cleared, the sea fell, the sun came out and dried our decks, and off we went like blithe schoolboys after a stiff exam., glad to be alive and done with it.

It was about this time that a pretty little brig came up and passed us in the morning watch. She was called the *Lucy*, of London. We never thought to see her again as she went dancing by, in all her bright new rig-out and the early sunlight about her, like a little sea fairy. But we did. And under the most tragic circumstances, too. I'll tell you all about her when I come to our next meeting. In the afternoon of the same day we caught our first shark. A beauty he was, fifteen feet long, or thereabouts. We got him with a hook like a boat's grapnel, baited with a four pound piece of beef.

We had brought a little pig from England with us, and christened him "Dennis." He became a great favourite. He knew his name and would come when any man called him. Well, we missed him during the storm, and when we opened Mr. Shark, behold, there was little Dennis "dead as cold pork," as the saying is, but never a toothmark on him. Johnny had bolted him whole. This sounds a little like Baron Munchausen, but it's an actual fact all the same. We buried the little thing reverently, I can tell you, wrapped in canvas, with a two-pound shot beside him, to make sure he wouldn't fall into the jaws of another of these pirates.

Then we arrived at Madeira, fifteen days out from Queenstown, and here I tasted my first banana (a great rarity in those days) and saw the little black boys diving for pennies. These kids can actually swim before they can walk. It was a treat to watch them. You would see the penny swirling down—down—down, and the little fellow, as brown as the penny itself, after it. Presently he would clutch the coin, into his mouth with it, and back again waiting for another to be thrown.

Here, too, I saw another sight that I've never forgotten: a woman swim out to the ship towing her baby by her breast. It hung over her shoulder and the youngster had the nipple in its mouth, holding on like grim death, and its little feet kicking out behind.

Four days we lay at Madeira, then went to Sao Vicente (we called it St. Vincent) in the Cape Verdes, for coal. Here we shipped our medical officer, Dr. Strickland, and here we had our first dinner of turtle. A most unpleasant, unpalatable dinner it was! The look of the green, slimy mess sickened me. But we soon got accustomed to it. Sailors will eat and grow fat upon anything. By and by our tastes became quite nice, and our stomachs craved for it—showing that, after all, Jack and My Lord High Admiral are brothers under the skin.

It was here, too, that an occurrence took place which caused a tremendous kick-up, both in the ship and ashore. It didn't happen on this, our first visit, but later. However, seeing we are at the place I may as well tell it now.

It was in December, and we expected to spend Christmas at sea. One of our fellows, Nobby Clark by name, a quiet, methodical sort of chap—a married man, too, by the way—had gone ashore to buy the provisions for all the four messes, but had been drugged by the storekeeper, a vile-looking Portugee, robbed of the money, stripped of his clothing, and then carried inland and left among the rocks. When the search party found him, eighteen hours afterwards, the poor soul was lying unconscious, with froth oozing from his mouth, and almost dead from exposure and the effects of the drug.

That Portugee was brought aboard, pretty nearly flayed alive by the bo'sun's mate, soused in the sea so that the brine would tickle him up a bit more, then taken ashore and handed over to the authorities.

We heard afterwards that they hanged the brute. Whether they did or not didn't matter to us, but I'll wager none in that cinder heap of an island ever wanted to interfere with a British bluejacket again.

Nobby gradually got better, and took a fair share of the Christmas dainties, but it was a long time before the shock of that affair completely left him.

After leaving St. Vincent, we struck the mainland and began the parade of our station. This went from Sierra Leone below the tenth parallel, right through that hot region, past Cape Palmas and the Ivory Coast, round Cape Three Points, and so along the Gold Coast to Cape Coast Castle, which was our headquarters.

There we rolled and rolled and rolled for a month at a stretch, scorched by its frizzling heat at one time, drenched by its roaring torrents of rain at another, and sometimes half killed by sudden downpours of hailstones as big as peanuts. When one of these showers came on, we youngsters would rush below, put on our black hats and come up and stand under it. It was glorious fun to hear the hail rattle on your hat, for all the world like a tune on the kettle-drum, and to see them go flashing off your mate's like crystal sparks from the Aurora Borealis.

The only relief to the tedium of this outlandish place was the arrival of the natives in their big war canoes. This usually happened two or three times a day. There would be twenty or thirty men in each, sitting along the gun'les, and they would come bounding over the sea—we lay a long way out on account of the heavy surf—brandishing their paddles and chanting their wild, weird litanies like people possessed. They always came singing.

They brought various kinds of fruit—bananas, pineapples, pomegranates, mangoes (all new to us then, but as common as apples nowadays)—yams, sweet potatoes, and other vegetables. Sometimes they brought "soft bread," which was made in small loaves, something like our morning rolls, each with a little green leaf adhering to it, but whether baked on it or not I forget.

They also brought articles made of ivory and wood, plaited reeds, and wonderful little trinkets in gold, such as bracelets, bangles, brooches, rings, etc. I bought a ring made from a piece of gold wire in the form of a true lover's knot, the joining of which was so well done that the doctor couldn't find the splice even with his microscope. Filigree work, too, so dainty and light that you could blow it about in your hand.

All these things they would barter for money or pieces of clothing; and the jabbering and shouting that went on during the bargaining was enough to awaken the dead. As a rule the natives were honest and very friendly, but even as a boy I thought it pitiful to see full grown men such as they were with no more intelligence than white children of eight or nine.

From Cape Coast Castle our beat went on past the Bights of Benin and Biafra, right through the Gulf of Guinea, passing the Island of St. Thomas on the Equator, and so down to the Cape of Good Hope.

It would be tedious to detail all the ports we touched at, even if I could remember them, so I will only mention the ones that have stuck to my memory through something of interest happening there.

For instance, the first time we touched Sierra Leone—then only a small cluster of huts, though a big place now, I believe—a big buck nigger came down to greet the boat, clad in a tattered pair of lady's stays, one old white gent's cuff, and a tile hat that would have disgraced a London cabby. But wasn't he proud!

At Freetown, Sierra Leone, we shipped our *kroomen*. These were negroes (liberated slaves), who were employed by the Navy for work in the sun. We had over a dozen. They lived under the fo'c'sle and some of them were choicely named. We had in our lot Jack Sunday, John Bull, Tom Pepper, Alfonso de Costa, Percy Montmorency, and—actually—Alfred Tennyson. Such is fame! Some of the missionaries could account for that, I daresay.

Jack Sunday was the patriarch of the tribe and used to conduct the religious services. He had a head of hair as curly as a mop and as white as the driven snow. He looked old, but was as nimble as a cat and did his work well. He had the manner of a judge and was as wise as Solomon. You could easily see Jack in the dark by reason of his white head, gleaming eyes and teeth.

John Bull was a huge fellow who well bore out his name. Tom Pepper was a clever artist and wood carver, and De Costa was the neatest at turning a turtle you ever saw. Indeed they were all clever and genial shipmates. One little fellow, Tom Walker, took a proper fancy to me and taught me a good bit of *Kroo* language.

They were all fine, natural singers, too. I never hear the hymns of Sankey, especially "Tell me the old, old Story," but back comes the fo'c'sle of the *Swallow* and these black, simple souls all blithely singing, in perfect time, the parts blending together like an organ, and old Jack Sunday wielding the baton with a dignity and bearing as grave as that

75

of the precentor leading the village choir.

The others watched him like hawks, following his every motion. If any of them went wrong he would shout "Now, den, younigga! Out wid dat note!"..."Not so high dar, you black fella!"..."Oh-h! I smiffligate you bym-bye!"...

Sometimes he would come down with the stick on one of their heads with a smack that would have broken a white skull, but the black man merely grinned and went on singing. They provided us with a nice little concert now and again and helped very much to keep the ship bright.

When we got into the cold weather south of the Line they used to dance about and breathe on their fingers, crying "Oh, massa—bite um, no see um!"

Mentioning St. Thomas on the Line reminds me of a pleasant hour. We had called there for some fresh spring water. It was during the tobacco harvest, and the flavour of the drying leaf came wafting out to sea to meet us. I never smell fresh tobacco but the scene of that lonely little island comes back to mind.

There I fell in with a Scotchman, named Mitchell, belonging to Peebles. He was foreman in one of the plantations; had been there twenty years, he told me, and was so delighted to meet a "brither Scot" that he took me up to his bungalow, treated me handsomely, and then sent me back aboard with half a dozen boxes of fine cigars. As we were allowed to light our pipes below then, the lower deck messes could hardly see each other for smoke, and the booby hatches used to belch like burning mountains.

The crossing of the Line (equator) for the first time was another event to remember. The day was given over absolutely to fun. An extra ration was served out in the morning and we had plum-duff for dinner at six bells (eleven o'clock). Twelve was the usual dinner hour, but on this day the Great Event took place at noon.

As eight bells struck, just when the sun was directly overhead, and you threw no shadow on the deck, Father Neptune, the Old King of Ocean, came aboard in high state attended by his court. The company consisted of His Majesty himself, his Secretary, Razor Bearer, Sword Bearer, Soap-boy, and a couple of mermaids. The king wore his crown and carried a huge, glittering trident. He was dressed in a flowing robe of seaweed and fish-scales, and with his long oakum beard, and face covered with barnacles, looked the funniest old Sea Monarch you could imagine. The attendants were dressed to correspond.

All we young sailors—three parts of the ship's company—clad in nothing but a pair of duck trousers, were brought before the king, duly presented by name, and given the freedom of the Seas thenceforth and forever according to ancient custom. We were well lathered with soap and slush, shaved, walloped over the head with the sword, and then capsized into a mighty bath which was rigged up in the space between the mainmast and the funnel-casing. Here the mermaids gave us a thorough sousing and then let us go—fully qualified seamen, initiated into all the Mysteries of the Deep.

A great ceremony! The maddest, merriest day I can recall!

In the evening the main brace was spliced—that is an extra tot of grog served out—and we finished up with a concert and some grand rolling choruses.

THE BIRTH OF A TURTLE

The islands of Ascension and St. Helena were also included in our beat and we visited them a number of times. Ascension lies in the middle of the Atlantic and is supposed to have taken its name from the suddenness of its arrival on this planet. It was said to have shot up in a night. It was used as a Naval depot, and here we came for stores.

A peculiar thing about this island was that the people didn't refer to the seasons as Spring, Summer, Autumn and Winter as we do, but as the Egg, the Turtle, the Fish and the Vegetable seasons. Great flights of Wide-awakes, a bird about the size of a seagull, came to lay their eggs in such droves that sometimes they actually hid the sun, while the air was raucous with their cries. They dropped their eggs on a wide plain called Wide-awake Fair, which in the season looked like a field of snow. The eggs lay in myriads, in some places over a foot deep. We used to take the jolly-boat ashore and bring off loads of them. It was great, keeping the birds off whilst collecting the eggs.

I remember a farm servant in the Perth district of Scotland telling me that he once lost a good fee through objecting to take salmon at every meal. The same objection must have been common at Ascension regarding turtle. Here these huge marine tortoises came in swarms to lay *their* eggs.

Mother turtle would waddle up the beach, her faithful mate following, scrape a hole in the sand, deposit her treasures, cover them up in a little mound, and then make for the water again. But just here the cunning islander intervened with a lasso, and the pair were given a trip inland to a large pond provided for them, and in this way the people had turtle all the year round.

The beach would be lined with these egg-mounds, and it was fascinating to watch the little turtle appear when the sun had hatched him. If you had the time and the patience to wait, or better still, the good fortune to be on the spot at the right moment to witness that sight—then you considered yourself lucky! The mound would seem to enlarge, the sand slip, and the first layer of eggs come to light.

Suddenly out would pop a small black head from a shell, a wee neck would crane, and you would see the head slowly rotate, taking a first, long, wondering view of its new surroundings. A short pause would ensue. Then you would see a convulsive heave, a wriggle, and out from the egg would flop master turtle, sit upon the sand for a minute, as if taking the air, and then make a bee-line for the water. As you saw the little creature breast the first wavelet licking the shore, you said to yourself, in the words of the psalmist, "*How wonderful are Thy works, O Lord!*"

In the fish season the water round the island simply teemed with fish—not that there was any great scarcity at any time, but at this particular time of year they swarmed—rock-cod, mullet and other kinds, that were as beautiful to look at and admire in the water as they were toothsome when brought from the pan.

Green Mountain, a hill not unlike Goatfell in Arran, was the only place where vegetation flourished on the island. All the rest was lava, slag, huge cones and mighty boulders. I am not sure if they had a hospital for the sick on Green Mountain at that time or were just going to build one, but I recollect that at the top of it there was a boat turned keel up that made a fine shelter from the fierce heat of the sun, and reminded one of Peggotty's house in *David Copperfield*.

They had also a little cemetery, but this was nearer the depot and was formed out of a dried-up lake with a surface like a billiard table. Some person of distinction was buried there, his headstone prominent among the other humble ones, but I can't remember who.

I liked coming to Ascension, there were so many interesting things about it—the "blow holes" out of which, far inland, the sea water would spout like fountains twenty feet high or so and break into spray; then the most beautiful "rainbows" you could imagine would form amid the spray, hang in the air a minute or so, then vanish; the strange rock-formations, and craters full of dark, motionless water, hiding you knew not what horrible devil-fish or tropical sea-monster. It was like a trip to the moon

An ideal cruising ground it was, too, for the chief purpose of the commission: *viz*, training for war. We got some fine practice in seamanship—which was just as necessary in those days as gunnery—at Ascension. We would take long spins out into the offing, go through any amount of evolutions, and back to our anchorage at night. Also we had the very best of gunnery practice here.

CHAPTER 14

Old Memories

When we started the commission, nearly every man on the lower deck began to keep a diary, but very few carried on the practice for any length of time. Before the ship was a year out, the craze had dropped till only one man, so far as I can remember, made anything like a systematic business of diary-keeping. This was Jack Durran, in No. 1 Mess. Jack filled five or six volumes—big, thick tomes they were, like grocers' day-books, with red and blue mottled edges and glossy covers—which would make particularly interesting reading now, I'll be bound, could they be got hold of.

Often and often I've regretted that I didn't continue the practice myself, but I was more taken up with skylarking and rhyme-making at that time than with such a useful pursuit as keeping a diary. I believe I had the gift, in a small way. But it wasn't till long years after that I woke to the fact of how useful such a pursuit as diary-keeping would have been to me had I started to develop it then.

But, *ochonerie*! As the Scotch song says, "*We're aye wise ahint the haun*."

I was blessed with a good memory, and was imaginative and enthusiastic, but not industrious. I was curious and questioning—I don't mean inquisitive—but I wanted to know things; was fairly intelligent—"*gleg o' the uptak*," as the saying is—and keen to know about and around and into the heart of everything that came under my notice. I remember I had one gift that was found very useful for a rainy hour under the fo'c'sle or down below: the gift of story-telling. For instance, I could retell a familiar incident, perhaps long after the event, and invest the yarn with a colour and interest that made it entertaining and agreeable, while holding fairly well to fact. This gift won for me the approbation of my mates, and, along with another little talent for reading aloud—very handy when the monthly parcel of books and periodicals which a few of us had subscribed for came out from England—and the ability to take part in any programme that was being made up, were about the only useful accomplishments I can lay claim to.

I could not sit down and write things, patiently day by day, as Jack Durran did. I rather stored them up and recalled them. Gloated over them. I do that yet.

What I took most delight in was rhyming. Poetry engrossed me. I read and mused over every scrap I laid hands on; and to turn out a "bit" myself seemed to me the very height of human achievement.

When an idea came into my head I would sit for hours pondering over the words, "the world forgetting" but not "by the world forgot," as a wet swab or a scrubbing brush would frequently testify. There's no scope for dreaming in the navy, goodness knows, and your mates aren't slow to keep you in mind of that fact; neither are the officers. Many a time, long after I was invalided, have I woke during the night with Billy's voice in my ears shouting: "Noble . . . Wool-gathering again" and turned over, thanking God it was only a dream.

This silly tendency to muse got me into no end of trouble. There is an enchantment about the sea—a beauty, a sparkle, a glamour that grips your senses and forbids you to think about anything but itself. The blueness of it, the brightness of it, the clearness, sweetness, freshness and ever-changing variety of it thrills and enthrals you. Who has words to describe the witchery of the sea? It puts you under a spell like a wizard and keeps you there. You simply cannot get away from it—at least that's how it got me.

Sometimes, when I was on the lookout, perched in the bunt of the foreyard, instead of looking out for ships, my mind would be away mooning over the colour of the water, the curve of a wave, the lift and fall of the bow, or the spray rising in cascades of glittering silver from the thrust of the forefoot. The wake, trailing away astern, spreading and spreading till it resembled a waving pathway leading to the stars, used to fascinate me. It was like looking back on life, with its ups and downs, its shadows and its bright spots. I would sit there, full of the wonder of it, dreaming, and forget to look about me and see if anything were in sight. The officer of the watch, seeing the lookout-man's gaze fixed intently astern, would stop his monotonous stumping of the poop, whip round, sweep the horizon with his glass, and finding nothing there, would bellow:

"Foreyard, there! . . . What the devil are you gaping astern in that booby fashion for? Look ahead!"

One day—how well I remember this—Mr. Daniells, the first lieutenant, came on deck and found a ship in full view that hadn't been reported. Of course I was on the lookout, and away in ba-ba dreaming about the gay times with all the pretty girls that were coming when the commission would be over, crooning to myself the words of "All's Well—"

And while his thoughts doth homeward veer,
Some well-known voice salutes his ear—

when a well-known voice from below saluted my ear with a jerk that nearly jumped me off the yard:

"Lookout, there! . . . Good God . . . Ah, it's you, Noble; at it again. Come down here, sir!" Then I caught it!

Seven days 10A (Admiralty punishment). Eat your grub under the 7-inch gun (and woe betide you if you left a mark on the deck). Grog stopped, leave stopped, holystoning, blacking-down, and all sorts of dirty work to do in the dog-watches and all your spare time. And, "unkindest cut of all," a black mark on your defaulter's sheet to be used against you at pension time.

I have often thought that there is a terrible lack of imagination, not to say humanity, in the "Rulers of the King's Navee," and that this black mark business is a poor commentary on their sense of justice. A man is barred from promotion, kept down in the pay list, branded as a criminal, sometimes for the pettiest of "crimes"—things which wouldn't be bothered about ashore. He not only does his punishment at the time, but, long years afterwards, when the sillinesses of youth are far behind, and he has done his duty faithfully and perhaps risen to distinction, up comes that black mark again and he finds his pension docked and the comfort of his declining years seriously interfered with.

Of course, the discipline of the Navy must be maintained, and nobody grumbles about being punished for offences committed; but there is something vindictive about this; something out of tune with the Service itself, whose main principles are camaraderie, *esprit de corps* and good-fellowship. There seems a meanness about this sort of treatment that recalls the days of Charles II, and makes a man feel that the country he has served faithfully and well, in spite of a few youthful errors, is not worth it.

What cured me of this bad habit of dreaming, however, was a skit which I wrote on Billy (the first lieutenant). It was Macaulay's "Virginia," one of the "Lays of Ancient Rome," that gave me the idea. It turned out a rare fo'c'sle ditty, and caused quite a furore in the ship. It dealt with an incident—but I believe the song itself will as readily explain the situation as a recital of the facts would, so I'll give you it.

Of course you must remember these were the days of the "long song." Some of them like "Windy Weather" had twenty or thirty verses, and, if they were extra good, as this old favourite was, would be sung and re-sung over and over again. We never seemed to tire of them. Mine had eleven, and a rolling, one-line chorus.

This is how it went:

Oh! Billyboy!
Ye toilers on the briney, with loyal hearts and true,
Come give me your attention and a tale I'll tell to you;
'Tis of the good ship Swallow, who merrily doth sail,
And before the fiercest hurricane can wag her pretty tail.

    Chorus: Oh! Billy! Billy, Billy bo-o-oy!

It is no paltry fiction I would to you unfold,
Of rain-drops turning into pearls, or fountains running gold,
But here, upon this vessel's deck, beneath the setting sun,
And right before our very eyes the crafty deed was done.

    Chorus: Oh! Billy! Billy, Billy bo-o-oy!

'Twas on a lovely evening, all in the days of yore,
Our gig's crew rowed an officer all safe from Afric's shore,
Where long they waited for him, in expectation keen,
Of getting each a pint of beer, drawn from our own canteen.

    Chorus: Oh! Billy! Billy, Billy bo-o-oy!

But when they reached the vessel, the beer had been served out,
And none being left for them, of course they had to go without,
So to reward those gallant hearts, and pacify their mind,
He promised each a glass of grog—and really it was kind!

    Chorus: Oh! Billy! Billy, Billy bo-o-oy!

When Billy reached his cabin he found his rum all gone,
But did he own it like a man? Oh no, not Number One!
But back he stump'd to where the four were standing, all agog,
A-waiting the command to go and drink his health in grog.

    Chorus: Oh! Billy! Billy, Billy bo-o-oy!

He turned him unto Maggar, and wrath was on his cheek,
He twisted in his monocle, and thus to him did speak:
"Oh, fie! you naughty sailor, for wearing dirty shoes!
You shan't have one until you've learnt to mind your P's and Q's!"

  Chorus: *Oh! Billy! Billy, Billy bo-o-oy!*

To Garter he said likewise: "You've in my favour sunk;
You can't have one, for well you know you have been getting drunk,
And till you mind your evil ways and better paths pursue,
A glass of grog I shall not give to any such as you!"

  Chorus: *Oh! Billy! Billy, Billy bo-o-oy!*

Then on a heel so jaunty, he left that gloomy twain,
But scarce had stepped six paces, when round he turned
again: "Ho, Kingsell! I'd forgotten; but, yet, 'tis not too late—
'Twas only yestermorn you disobeyed the gunner's mate."

  Chorus: *Oh! Billy! Billy, Billy bo-o-oy!*

"And think you I'd be blameless in giving you a glass?
No, sir! and well you know it—stand aside and let me pass!
For trouble you've been making, on your name there is a blot,
And if you'd have it taken off—go clean your dirty shot."

  Chorus: *Oh! Billy! Billy, Billy bo-o-oy!*

To little Tommy Logan he said in accents clear:
"You'll get your glass tomorrow, but not today, my dear."
But Billy, dearest Billy! you surely have forgot,
For little Tommy Logan is still without his tot!

  Chorus: *Oh! Billy! Billy, Billy bo-o-oy!*

So now, my poor old comrades, I pray you do not frown,
Nor give your hearts to sorrow, though Billy's turned you down;
But think upon the moral: that promises are vain,
And never trust an officer who wears a window-pane!

  Chorus: *Oh! Billy! Billy, Billy bo-o-oy!*

The tune was a great favourite in ships' fo'c'sles in my time. It was sung to "The Sunny fields of Spain," "The female cabin-boy," and one or two others. My words clinked to every note of it, and the song "took on" immensely. I think I see the fellows beating time and waiting for the last word of each verse and then coming in: "Oh! Billy," etc.

The last verse was the favourite. It was trolled out with special gusto. But the whole song was hugely enjoyed on the lower deck and highly applauded, for Billy was not very well liked. I came in for a good deal of praise and back-clapping,

And lived the hero of my little hour,

but, oh dear me, the glory was transient!

Fred Booth, one of our signalmen—a very clever shipmate—actor, singer, artist—I have two of his pictures in my house to this day—and general "Jack-of-all-trades"—a proper handyman was Buntin—got me persuaded into lending him the little book in which all my precious "poems" were inscribed. He promised faithfully to keep it to himself and let nobody see it. But, alas! Buntin's word was as brittle as Billy's—perhaps the temptation was too strong to resist—I don't blame him. What I should have done was to have lived up to my own teaching by being chary of promises. Anyway, Fred took the book aft and showed it to Mr. Baynham, the navigating lieutenant, and the Master was so tickled that he read the entire contents aloud in the wardroom, "to the great glee of the rest of the officers," as I heard afterwards.

When I found this out I was so disgusted that I flung the book over the side and vowed to rhyme no more.

But it was too late. Billy got hold of the name of the author of the song, and from that night till the end of the commission his knife was in me.

While I was writing my doggerel, I had no idea of what I was doing—that I was committing the most heinous crime in the Naval decalogue—the unpardonable sin of holding an officer up to ridicule, and he the commanding officer of the ship in which I was serving as a humble O.D. That aspect of the affair never struck me. What I thought was: "This is going to be a fine old 'Come all ye,' with a roaring chorus that will please the boys." And I really couldn't help myself. The words just came . . . and I wrote them down . . . and the tune fitted . . and—there you are!

But I was made to think plenty about the other side later on. It is a serious thing to incur the ill-will of your superior officer, mind you! Billy, although not actively hostile, and while pretending to treat the matter lightly, never let a chance slip to get me all the same. And he got me often. Many a time was my nose rubbed in the mire through that glorious blunder.

Once when we were alone on the fo'c'sle together, he said, in a voice that sheared into me like the stroke of a cutlass:

"You devil! It's not now I'll punish you; its later on. Years after this you'll think about me all right!"

And he was as true as his word! Though I was anxious to get on, and did get on fairly well for the time I was in the Service, and left it at last, I'm proud to say, with "Exemplary"—the high-water mark of good character—on my discharge certificate; and while I managed to put a good few black marks on that sheet before referred to by my own thoughtless stupidity, Billy undoubtedly helped me to a good many more which I might easily have escaped.

And now, they tell me he has gone over to the Great Majority, while here I am still "Years after," as he said, left to "think about" him. I wonder if the thoughts he has caused me to think are any comfort to him now. Poor Billy!

Ah, well,

> The evil that men do lives after them,
> The good is oft interred with their bones.

However, "In spite of all my troubles, I was glad," as the song says. I liked the life, I liked my shipmates, and I liked my ship. I liked the Navy as well for the romance surrounding it as for the life itself—the open air, the variety, the charm of change, of seeing new faces and new places, living with companions who thought as I did, spoke as I did, and had the same outlook on life as I had myself. It was glorious.

Mr. Routh, the second lieutenant, who was also the officer of my division, was a splendid young fellow, one of the kind you hear men say they "would go to hell with—or for." Open, frank, good natured, and free-handed with his money. A true sailor. Many a half-crown he handed to us men on the quiet when we were hard up, and never a pay-back would he hear of.

I always think of Mr. Routh as the perfect type of naval officer. A bold, intrepid, daring fellow, ready for anything. Game, romp or race, fun, fight or frolic—there was Routh, always at the front, and always the gentleman.

A great sportsman, too. When a sporting stunt was on and he called for volunteers to go with him, every man in the ship jumped to the call, and "clover" wasn't in it compared to what you thought of yourself if you were lucky enough to be picked.

And a rare kind-hearted lad. I remember one night, after the arrival of the mail which had brought me bad news from home, he came to me at the wheel and asked me kindly if anything was the matter. He said he had noticed that I was unusually quiet all day, and hoped things were all right in Scotland.

I thanked him, and said it was my mother—she was rather poorly just now; but didn't go into details.

He went away, but came back in a minute and shoved two sovereigns into my hand, saying:

"Send her these, Noble; maybe they'll help. Now, not a word!"

He must have divined the trouble, for money was just the thing needful.

Another night when we were ploughing through a heavy sea and a cold sleety drizzle, surrounded by

Voices of moaning winds and threatening thunders,

he got me at the wheel again, and asked if I would like a smoke.

"Ah, wouldn't I just, sir!"

"Very well, light up. If I hear the captain stir I'll give a tap on the deck."

This wasn't favouritism. Other fellows had the same experience as myself.

Ah! Routh was a rare one. If success came by good wishes he would be a Lord High Admiral by now, for not a soul in the ship but wished him well. As for me—my eyes fill to this day when I think about him.

CHAPTER 15

The Skipper

The Captain, John Borlase Warren, was one of the finest men that ever breathed. Strict on duty, but an honest, fair-minded gentleman for all that. He never punished a man on the day he was taken up before him, but always delayed sentence till the day following, so that he could think the "crime" over and give the man fair-play. If there was any doubt, the man got full benefit of it.

And he hated toadying—simply loathed it. He dismissed a whole batch of defaulters one day—I was one of them, and mighty glad I was about it—because the bo'sun's mate, who had a man up for some breach of discipline, adopted a wheedling tone and used too many "yes, sirs" and "no, sirs" and "d'ye see, sirs?"

The skipper looked at the P.O. with his lip curling. Then he snatched his cap from his head, dashed it on the deck—a habit he had when irritated—and burst out:

"Silence, sir! How dare you speak to me in that fashion!—Go away! Dismiss everything! I'll have nothing of that kind in this ship"—and off he stumped to his cabin, the ship's corporal running after him with his cap.

He was sharp as a needle at an evolution or at drill, and saw everything. He had only one eye; the other had been lost in some scrap in the Baltic, I heard, but we used to say he had four: two in front, one at the back, and one at the top of his head. He was quick to notice a flaw in a man, and to point it out to him in a sensible way, and just as quick to see a good point and praise him for it.

Talk about faithfulness to duty! I have known him keep the bridge during a storm that ran its miserable length into weeks; when the galley fire was washed out and life was Desolation itself. Hardly ever going below, but just having a bite brought to him by the steward. At such a time, if you were inclined to grumble or think yourself ill-used, a glance at the poop would steady your nerves and set you right in a twinkling.

If you happened to be at the wheel, or in the chains, or on the look-out, you would sense him "going the rounds," unseen and speaking to nobody. But you knew he was there, watchful and vigilant, and felt that the safety of the ship was in capable hands; that God was in his Heaven, and all was right with the world. And the thought bucked you up tremendously and made you stick to your guns for all you were worth.

We all liked him. Here is one of the little touches that went a long way towards winning that regard. It shows the real kind of stuff the skipper was made of.

We used to have salt beef ("salt 'oss" we called it) twice a week at sea for dinner. Some of this stuff was so old that nobody could tell its age. On one occasion a cask of beef was actually discovered in our hold, whose mark and tally dated it back to Trafalgar! At another time, one of my messmates cut a half-model of a frigate out of a piece, sand-papered, varnished, and then glued it to the ship's side above the bread-barge. You couldn't have told it from mahogany. We carried that trophy home with us.

Well, one day when the salt beef was brought from the galley, the smell of it filled the lower deck and set all hands coughing. It was a strange smell—a heavy, musty, ancient sort of odour, suggesting graveyards and cathedral crypts, and that the beef must have been in the cask since the creation of the world. It was the kind of flavour you would expect an Egyptian mummy to give off if it were boiled. . . . Ugh! . . . Of course there was a row. A proper shindy took place in the galley, and "Old Umbray" (our pet name for the cook) was nearly eaten alive. I was at the wheel at the time, waiting for my relief, and heard it. By and by, along came the whole of No. 4 Mess, the one I belonged to, headed by Ginger White, with the smoking mess-tin, to see the captain. The men lined up on the quarter-deck. Just then, Curly Millet, the captain's steward, came from the galley carrying the captain's dinner on a dish with a cover on it. The officer of the watch—I think it was Mr. Routh—came down from the poop, questioned the men—and didn't take long about it, either, after one sniff—and then knocked at the cabin door.

Out came the skipper. "Well men," he said, "what's the trouble?"

Ginger White showed the meat, with his nose screwed up.

The skipper took a sniff and then blew his breath out. "Phew! Steward!" he called. "Just bring my dinner out here, will you? Bring table and all, just as it is."

Millet did as directed, and laid the table, on which was a plate with a little round cover, another with a few pieces of ordinary ship's-tack (biscuits), a glass of water and a table-napkin, down almost close to Ginger's bare feet.

You would have thought some conjuring trick was about to be performed.

"Now," said the skipper to Ginger, "lift the cover, will you?"

Ginger handed his dish to Sharkie Redford, who was standing nearest to him, and did as he was told.

"Smell it," said the captain. "Take the plate in your hand and smell it."

Ginger did so, and crinkled his nose afresh. Then he replaced the cover, saluted, snatched his dish from Sharkie's hands, wheeled round, and without a word tramped back to the lower deck, followed by the crowd. The skipper's dinner was exactly the same as our own. That was Captain Warren all through.

Another anecdote, characteristic of the captain. We were lying anchored off a Dutch Settlement up one of the African rivers—the Congo or the Niger, I forget which. Neither do I recall the name of the place. It is so long ago, and the names of these African towns are so outlandish, that it is difficult for British lips to speak them, let alone keep them in memory.

Anyway, the place swarmed with crocodiles. We could see them basking on the sand-banks, or lying side by side with the huge logs of mahogany that were collected on the river bank in front of the village. Great, hideous brutes they were, with long, pointed heads, and mouths like yawning gateways, furnished with a double portcullis of greedy, yellow teeth.

There they would lie, as like a log as you could imagine and as motionless, waiting for a chance child to come and play among the wood, as children do all the world over. Then there would be a snap, a blood-curdling yell, a commotion among the logs, and down the pair of them would go. Once we actually saw a child rescued from the very jaws of one of these monsters. A crocodile had got hold of him, but the father, who happened to be near, plunged into the water and forced the brute to drop its prey. *How* he did it, I don't know; but he *did*, and the youngster was saved.

One afternoon, Tom Carter, belonging to the "side-party," was slung over the bows in a bo'sun's-chair, giving the ship a touch up, when he lost his balance and fell into the water. Three or four of us were working in the waist, washing down. I had just flung over the bucket for another dip (a breach of the side-party's rules that Carter himself would not have been slow to make a noise about, but a providence for him then!), when the skipper, who was walking the poop, cried:

"Waist there! Look after that man."

We all sprang to the side, and there was Tom's head bobbing in the fast-moving current. Dolly Brown, who had hold of the line, pulled up the bucket, jerked it empty and swung it forward to meet Tom, then gradually drew in the slack, saying to us: "Stand by to hoist him up."

All of a sudden the skipper cried excitedly: "Pull, men! Up with him! For God's sake, quick!"

Automatically we fell back on the line and up came Tom's head over the entry port, like a Jack-in-the-box, followed by a splutter in the water alongside. We bundled him in and looked over. There we saw a beauty of a croc, pawing the water, in the attitude of a dog "begging," with a mouth like a jail door, his jaws working for all the world like a pair of gigantic scissors.

Dolly cried "Damn your eyes!" and flung the bucket right down his throat, and the brute made off with it, carrying away the lanyard. Then the skipper cried from the brake of the poop:

"Carter! Down on your knees, sir, and thank God for your deliverance. . . . Down with you!"

Never, surely, ascended to heaven from a ship's deck a more fervent expression of gratitude than when poor Carter, in a voice trembling with emotion, ejaculated "Thank God! Oh! Thank God!"

The captain came down and congratulated him on his escape— which you will admit was a narrow one—patted his shoulder, and then he told him to go below and shift, and after that to go to his (the captain's) steward, and a glass of grog would be waiting him, and altogether carried through this rather exciting business in a manner that endeared him to the whole ship's company.

He instituted a Savings Bank (an uncommon thing in those days), started a (weekly) Penny Readings night, and contributed himself; giving us such pieces as *The Demon Ship*, and *The Sailor's Apology for his bow-legs*, from Hood, who seemed to be his favourite author. He also brought aboard Mr. Hopkins, who was British Consul for the West Coast, and the finest reader of Dickens I ever heard. How we laughed over Sergeant Buzfuz, and "The lady with yellow curl-papers." Booby Grey, a messmate of mine, fell off the main fife-rail one night laughing, and nearly broke his own head and the head of the man sitting below him. Those were fine nights!

CHAPTER 16

The Bo'sun

The officer of the lower deck was the Bo'sun, Mr. Freedie. "Tommy" we called him, or "Pipes." He is another I carry a fine memory of.

He was a big man, muscular and hairy, with a hand like a deckbucket and a voice like the Archangel Gabriel. Nobody could say they didn't hear him. If he wanted anything, and shouted for you, and he were on the fo'c'sle and you in the hold, you heard him all right. And swear! We used to say he made the ship's candles burn blue. But it was done in such a cheery, hearty fashion, and came out so round and in such volume, and with such honest goodwill, that we rather admired this special gift of his than took offence at it. We knew he meant no harm. He hadn't a wide vocabulary, to be sure, but oh! it was pithy, and flowed like a stream.

The best of it was he didn't know he was swearing. He really didn't. I remember one day the foreyard men were doing something aloft, and Tommy was conducting operations and in great form. All of a sudden, Billy, who was standing by, cried out: "Oh, Mr. Freedie, Mr. Freedie! Don't use such abominable language!"

Tommy pulled up as if he had been shot.

"Beg pardon, sir. Language, what language, sir?"

"Why the language you are using, it's enough to sink the ship!"

Tommy grinned, while the men looked down, enjoying the interlude.

"Why, bless ye, sir," he said—his hairy face glowing with good humour, and looking aloft with a "the-Lord- loveth-whom-he-chasteneth" sort of expression—"why, bless ye, they don't mind. That's all right. They knows all about that, sir. It ain't nothing."

"Ah, but you must not use such language. I will not have it. It's most disgusting," the first lieutenant replied emphatically, and walked aft.

I think I see the look of pity the bo'sun flung after him as he touched his cap and answered: "Ay, ay, sir. Very good."

He waited a minute or so to let the officer as far out of hearing as possible, then turned to the crowd above. "Now, then, you Saltash fishwives!" he roared, nearly choking with the restraint he had put upon himself, "D'ye hear that? you d-d- *darlings!—You know!—*You d-d-dear ones!—you know what I mean! Come on, you d-d-doddering dockyard mateys! You, you—I'll teach you! I'll teach you, you b-b-*beauties—*you know! —to get me into a row. Come on; up with that bunt. D'ye hear—you, you"—squinting aft and shaking his fist—"Just wait a bit!"

It was a treat to listen to him.

Nobody knows what torture it was to hold himself in while the first lieutenant was about. But when he had the deck to himself—!

For all that, Tommy Freedie was as fine an officer as a man could wish to sail with. A true, honest sailor-man. Bluff and loud of speech, rough and forbidding in appearance, but under the skin a proper heart of corn.

We "youngsters"—there were six or seven of us—went in mortal fear of him, for his boot was as ready as his hand—such a hand! —and he always carried a rope's end in his pocket.

But after a month or two, we took him in the day's work and just shied clear of him. At working ship or sail-drill his station was forward, and as I was a main-t'-gallant-man I didn't come under his scope. Billy was my officer. But, with all Tommy's rough ways, I would blithely have exchanged Number One for him any day.

My chum during the whole four years of the commission was a boy named Jack Belton. William was his real Christian name, but somebody had christened him "Jack," and "Jack" he stayed to the end.

How I loved that boy! And what grand chums we were! We shared everything together; and as we were in opposite watches we were able to do many a little service for one another. We argued and brawled perpetually, for in some ways our habits of mind were as different as the poles. It was quite common to hear one of the older men shout "Now, then, you two!" or "Oh, go and bury yourselves!" and a wet dishclout would come flopping around our ears. Sometimes we got kicked out of the mess altogether for making a row.

But for all our wrangling we loved each other like David and

Jonathan. What was Jack's was mine, and mine his. We had the run of each other's ditty-boes, read each other's letters, shared each other's secrets, ambitions, and so forth, fought with and for each other, were altogether a good pair of sea chums. The beggar got the better of me in many a bout, for he was a bigger and stronger lad than I; but I don't think, looking back now, that either of us could claim to have had the weather side of the other. I love that lad yet. Even now my heart thrills at the remembrance of him, and I would give something to feel his hand in mine again. But I doubt that will never be.

CASTLES IN SPAIN

Jack and I were among the first batch of Ordinary Seamen passed for the rate of A.B. (Able Seaman) by Mr. Freedie, the bo'sun. I shall not forget that experience if I live to be a much older man than I am today. This is how it came about.

One night in the first dog, Jack and I were leaning over the fo'c'sle-rail watching a shoal of porpoises capering round the bows like a crowd of schoolboys in a playground. These sea-pigs are a great divert, and cause endless interest and amusement. They frisk and gambol in front of the ship for miles, their lean black bodies rolling and tumbling over and under each other, sometimes leaping right over the crest of a wave, or rushing about in all directions with a swishing noise, like water under a mill-wheel, and making the most wonderful figures you could think of, like a skater on an ice-pond, which the phosphorescence of the sea, especially at night, turns into a display like fireworks.

We used to watch them often; and the dolphin launching his graceful, brightly-coloured length, like a gleaming torpedo, after the flying fish; and the flying-fish themselves rising with a splutter out of the sea and whirring along for a couple of hundred yards or so and then falling in again; and the albatross planing overhead with never a motion of his wing—these and countless other sights, all strange and beautiful, we used to watch and admire for hours together.

This evening, having the deck to ourselves, I broached a subject that had been in my mind for a day or two.

"Jack," I said, all of a sudden, "what do you say to going in for able seaman?"

Jack started. "What's that, Jock?" (Scotsmen, I may mention, are called either "Jock," "Sandy," or "Mac," in the Navy, never by their real names.)

I repeated the question.

Jack looked round at me, with his face wrinkled into a grin. "Fine able seamen we should make, shouldn't we?"

"Well," I returned, "I don't know, we haven't tried yet."

"G' 'way! Why, we were only rated O.D.'s the other day."

"Well," I said; "we managed that all right, didn't we? What's to hinder us taking a step higher?"

Jack looked straight at me. "Are you joking?"

"No!" I said, with my brows down; "what's there to joke about?"

"Because if you're serious, you're silly. Why, man alive, we're too young."

"Oh," says I, "that's easily got over: we'll be older tomorrow.

"So we will," he answered, and laughed. "But, here, how about the other fellows? There's any amount of ordinary seamen in the ship already before us."

"Oh, well, Jack," I said, "as to that, if they like to stick O.D.'s all their lives that's no reason why we should."

Jack shook his head. I wasn't sure about it myself for, as he said, there were a good few of our shipmates who had been much longer in the Service and were still ordinary seamen.

It was a bold thought, anyway. No harm could come of letting it soak in, and mighty relieved I was in getting it off my chest.

We took a stump up and down the deck for a while, and were back again at the rail looking at the flying figures ahead, when Jack gripped my arm hard, and said in an awed whisper, "Here, Jock! How about Tommy?"

This brought my heart into my mouth, and caused us both to sit down on the hen-coop and look at one another in dismay. D'ye know, I felt the hair rise on my skull. This was an act in the play that I had never even given a thought to. To face our mates was a big thing, without a doubt. But to face Tommy—oh, Lord! . . . A cold tingling crept down my spine! I sat for a minute or two on the hen-coop looking blankly at my chum, feeling that the bottom had been completely knocked out of my scheme by his remark. There was a twinkle in Jack's eye which suggested that the humorous side of the situation appealed to him. But there was no fun in it for me.

It was all very well for Jack, whose people were fairly well off, to lie back and let the wind blow him along. But it was different with me. I had been looking the matter over from a financial point of view and saw clearly what the step meant for me if I could win it. Here was the position.

In my time, when a boy in the Navy reached the age of eighteen he was rated Ordinary Seaman (O.D.) right off, and his pay was one shilling a day. That came to him automatically, on account of his age. But if he managed to pass an examination in seaman-ship, not a very hard one, he was "made" First Class Ordinary Seaman, and his pay raised to one and three-pence.

An Able Seaman (A.B.) drew one and seven-pence, and if he were also "Trained Man"—a distinction gained by passing a preliminary examination in gunnery—that brought in another penny a day, making it one and eight.

Jack and I had jumped from the boy-rating to First Class O.D. some time previously; consequently our daily screw was one and three. Reaching the A.B. Trained Man rate meant another five-pence. Five-pence a day meant something near two pounds extra a quarter, and that sum (to me) opened up great possibilities, not to mention the glory of having "A.B." on your letters from home.

Besides, how I knew the dear little woman in Scotland would dance for joy to hear of my promotion! And how her share of the proceeds, little though it was bound to be, would help to lighten her lot! I could picture her while my eye fell on the shimmering water ahead, and with the noise of the playing porpoises in my ears—Lord, how often her sweet old face swam into my vision during those four lonely years!—I could picture her trudging to her work in the mill every morning at six o'clock, fair weather or foul, and none knew better than I how much an extra shilling or two would add to her comfort when the long, dreary, twelve-hour day was done.

And the girl! The little maid in the blue frock, with her arms bare from above the elbow, her soft, brown eyes and the two auburn plaits hanging down her back, who looked so sweet and cool and bonnie as we sat on the green slope of the Barrack Park that memorable evening just before my last leave was up. What a joy it would be to send her a trinket now and again just to keep the flame burning! I corresponded with her regularly, filling reams of paper telling her all about the places we touched at, the black people and their strange manners and customs so different from our own, and all the wonderful things we saw or heard about.

She worked in the mill, too—I used to work beside her as "oiler," before I went to sea—and I could fancy her taking the things I sent her down to the flat and showing them off to the other girls, who

97

would go into raptures over them and envy her the possession of such a fine sailor-boy. And who knew what might happen when I came home with my blue reefer and bell-bottoms on, and my pocket crammed full of money when the commission was over.

And fancy popping in among my old chums in Dundee, with maybe a couple of gold badges and the cross anchors and crown blazing on my left arm. They would still be "mull-fuds," poor fellows! and had seen nothing. Wouldn't I warm their ears with the tales I would tell 'em.

Lord! Lord! those pictures!

When I looked up from my day-dreams I found Jack still regarding me with the same old humorous twinkle, now broadened into a grin. I gave him one in the ribs which tumbled him off the hen-coop, and there would have been a fight—sure, had not the bo'sun's mate at that minute piped "Watch, trim sails!" It being Jack's watch on deck he had to look slippy; which he did, saying as he went, "You wait!"

However, there was no further chance of discussion that night. The next day a spell of bad weather set in, and we had no time for anything but drying wet clothes and attending to our various duties.

Then one day in the dinner hour Jack got hold of me, and said quietly, "Jock, I'm with you."

"Good for you, old chummy!" I said joyfully. "Now we'll manage! How will we set about it?"

"Oh, well; we'll have to see Tommy first, of course. But he can't eat us, can he?"

"Not he," I answered (but I said to myself, "He'll take a good bite, anyway!")

"Here," I went on, and slipped my arm through his. "D'ye know, I've been thinking this business inside out"— Jack nodded. "So have I"—"and I have the feeling that if we get him in a good humour . . . Savvy?"

"Savvy it is; that's exactly what I think," said Jack, squeezing my arm, as keen now as I was myself. . . . "What do you say to looking him up this evening after drill?"

"The very thing! Then we'll get it over. . . . The sooner the better."

That was settled.

Passing for A.B.

Thus it was that in the dog-watch two trembling sailor-boys crept down the lower deck towards where the bo'sun's cabin was situated, and after shuffling about for a little knocked at the door.

"Come in!" roared a bull voice.

Jack nudged me on to the door-knob, but I hastily drew back, rattling it as I went, and pulled him forward, and the ship giving a roll, he fumbled up against the door and shook it.

"Come in!" roared the voice again. "Who the devil's that? Can't you open the door and come in?"

Now for it!

Jack and I knitted our teeth and looked grimly at one another. Then I made a hesitating movement to catch hold of the handle, but Jack shoved me on one side, grabbed it, and opened the door a little. But another roll coming, I had just time to glimpse the bo'sun sitting below the scuttle with his sleeves up and a book in his hand, when it shut to again with a bang.

We hung in the wind a minute, undecided whether to run or stand. Jack's face queried in consternation, "Did he see you?" I nodded energetically.

"Heavens above!" yelled Tommy. "Who the blazes is that monkeying at my cabin door? Will you come in, or sh'll I come and pull your liver out?"

It was like the roar of a lion. I felt my legs shake under me and would have given worlds for the deck to open and drop me in among the rats in the hold. Jack told me afterwards that his feelings were the same as mine. But we had no time to compare notes then. It was Hobson's Choice for the pair of us. He pulled the door open again, I took a blind step forward, and forgetting to lift my foot clear of the coaming, plunged headlong into the cabin.

Tommy had been spending a luxurious hour in reading, and his feet were spread out when I went sprawling in beside them. He jerked them back like lightning. I had a horrible fear that he meant to kick out, and bounded to my own again with the spring of an ante- lope, and stood panting against the bulkhead. Jack, profiting from my mishap, entered more sedately, and when I looked round, was standing gaping just inside the door in the attitude of somebody who is waiting for something dreadful to happen.

Tommy clashed down the book on a little chest of drawers at his elbow, and gripped the sides of his chair as if he were going to spring at us. But seeing who we were, and the little box of a place being full, he just rose, stretched out his big hand, swung Jack alongside of me, and thundered: "Holy milkman!"

This was a favourite prelude of his when something special in the way of sea-rhetoric was coming—"Holy milkman! . . . What the hell d'ye mean by this? . . . You young devils! . . . Are you out skylarking? . . . What's the idea . . . disturbing a man's peace . . . when he's taking a quiet rest . . . like this, eh?" At every pause he knocked our heads together till our teeth rattled. "Out with it! . . . . Come on! . . . What are you up to?"

He glowered at us both, but neither of us could open our lips, we were so terrified.

"Can't you speak?" he bellowed. "Come on! What's in the wind? . . . Shut that door! "

Jack flew to obey him, and I blurted out "Nothing, sir; really nothing. We were just calling on you!"

Tommy looked terribly big and fierce when he was angry. His arms and chest were covered with hair, and when he had hold of us, Jack and I felt like a couple of laths in the hands of a mighty harlequin. I believe he could have swung the pair of us round his head if he'd had a mind. But he wasn't cruel. No! Anything but that! Under the surface he had a rare kind heart, and this sentence of mine seemed to have shot straight into it. For when Jack, having closed the door, sidled up to me again, he was back in his chair with his arms folded, and the look in his face of a father who had been compelled to put two of his unruly boys through the mill but had now forgiven them.

"Ay," he said, "so you have just come to call on me, eh? . . . And what are you calling on me about?"

We both began to speak at once, but he stopped us, and I being nearest to him, he nodded to me and said curtly, "You launch out."

I said we had to come to ask if there would be any objection to us going in for A.B.

The bo'sun lifted his eyebrows but said nothing.

I then told him that we had been thinking about it for some time; that we were eager to get on in the Service, keen to try for the rate, but we didn't know very well where to begin. That we had no books beyond our Manual which, though good enough in its way, didn't go far enough. We felt there were others that might be of even greater service to us, and we came to him thinking that he might advise us as to what books to get and where to get them.

"Above all, sir," I said, for I was now warm, and I could see he was interested, "we thought if we could manage to win your sympathy and a hint now and again, perhaps the loan of a book, while we're working our way through . . . we feel about certain we'll succeed."

Where the words came from I don't know, but they came all right, pat, and without any bother. During the recital I felt Jack's arm press into my side, so I knew I was doing well.

When I had finished, I thought the bo'sun would kick us out of the cabin for our cheek. Instead of that, he never moved or spoke, but lay back and seemed to be surveying us both: sort of taking our measure, for about a minute. Then he drew up his legs again and said: "Well, I'm damned . . . Well, I'm tee-tee-totally damned! . . . Aren't you the two youngsters that I passed for Ordinary Seamen not long ago?"

"Yes, sir."

"And now you want to be Able Seamen, eh?" he said, rubbing his chin with the back of his hand.

He appeared to be thinking aloud.

"What mess are you in?"

We told him.

"Do the others know about this?"

"No, sir."

I saw him cast a look at our shoulders where the watch-stripes were displayed, and knew he was noting that we were in opposite watches.

He asked a few more questions, such as—when we joined the Service, and where; which training ship we came from, and so forth. Some technical ones he put to us also: how this, that and the other was done. But though his manner had lost a lot of its gruffness, we couldn't tell from his face what he thought of the answers.

All at once he stood up, laid a hand on a shoulder of each of us, and said, "Now, d'ye know what I think?" (I thought to myself, "Here it comes!") "Did you ever hear what the devil said to his nostrils"—drawing the word out—"when he blew the candle out with 'em?"

"No, sir," we answered, wondering what on earth was coming now.

"Well," he said, "you're a biddy good pair!—that's what he said. And that's what I think. I think you're a pair of right plucky kids and I like your spirit. I didn't give the lower deck the credit for having so much grit—damn me if I did! Now, look here."

He told us what we were to do. We were to start right off at once; say nothing to anybody; he would provide what books we should need; be our guide, philosopher and friend, and help us in every way he could think of. Whatever trouble we got into we were to bring it to him and he would smooth it away—all this he said in his deep rumbling voice, with some good advice thrown in, patting us kindly on the shoulders the while, like a rough, bluff, gruff old uncle organizing a treat in which we were to be the principal sharers, not at all the big-toothed curmudgeon we expected he would be. I tell you we felt fine! It would have been a joy to have taken his hairy old face—not so very old in years either—in our arms and kissed it. I felt my heart glow within me. Often and often have I experienced the same feeling since, and blessed the name of Tommy Freedie, so great a thing is it for a boy to meet a kindred soul in one of his elders placed in authority above him.

"But," he concluded, "bear in mind you'll have to work—work like blazes.... God Almighty help you if you don't! ... Now clear out and let me get on with my yarn."

He shepherded us out of the cabin and closed the door. Jack and I stood outside it a minute and silently embraced each other in ecstasy. Then we flew up the ladder and on deck like streaks of greased lightning, leap-frogged along the waist as far as the tub-house, and raced back to the fo'c'sle again as if in the Seventh Heaven.

The bo'sun manfully kept his word. And a more patient, easy-to-get-on-with teacher no boy ever had—although, of course, he didn't forget to mingle a cuff with his coaching now and then. And he would admit, I'm sure, if he ever gave the incident a thought, that no teacher ever had a pair of pupils more enthusiastic or willing to learn than my dear old chum and I. Anyway, in about three months' time he judged us fit for the examination, and I'm glad to remember we passed with colours flying, the gunnery-test for T.M. as well, and even won a word of praise from the captain.

CHAPTER 17

The Doctor

I remember the doctor with pleasure. He was a tall, dignified gentleman—young, not thirty, with a gracious presence and an extra sweet smile—it lit up his whole face. The very look of him brought comfort to us when we were ill. He was writing a book, so I heard. I hope he made something by it. Many a book he lent me. That, however, by the way.

Very little serious illness came to the *Swallow*. We were always blessed with good health, and this I attribute to the care and skill of Dr. Strickland and the wise precautions he took to prevent illness. For instance, he had no sooner stepped aboard at *St. Vincent* than up went a notice on the lower deck blackboard, warning the ship's company against the fish that swam alongside. Indeed, for the whole four years, we had only one case that ended in death. This was the captain's steward, a Japanese, who took coast fever; but even him the doctor would have pulled through had the man reported sick earlier than he did.

This man's death affected us greatly. There was an awe about it, a suddenness that struck the entire ship's company and settled on the lower deck like a cloud for a time. He was the first to be taken. We knew him intimately, and liked him—a quiet, earnest-looking, soft-footed little chap.

Yesterday we had been talking to him; today he was dead. And his life had gone out in agony—so Bunthorne, the sick-bay steward, told us.

Personally, the incident made a tremendous impression upon me. It was my first experience of death, and it was also my first funeral at sea. I remember the solemn scene at the gangway: The captain reading the service for the dead; the figure on the grating, sewn up in his hammock, with the two round shot at his feet, and covered by the Union Jack; his sorrowful shipmates all gathered around, and everybody dressed in white; the tropical sun blazing overhead and bringing sparks from a ring on the captain's little finger; the ship under full sail sliding through the blue water with scarcely a sound, and the air of reverent attention on every face. I particularly remember the rumble and the appalling splash when, at the words "*We therefore commit his body to the deep*," the grating was tilted and our poor shipmate took the final plunge. It sent a thrill through me that I feel the tingle of even now as I write. And I also remember thinking to myself "How glad I am that I left the mill and came to sea! When would that squalid existence have provided an incident calling up such thoughts as are now lifting my soul to heaven!" It was a great and wonderful experience for a lad.

A peculiar case happened at Elephant Bay, a lovely spot somewhere around the mouth of the river Niger, where we had gone to have the ship fumigated after the death of the captain's steward.

Here an ordinary seaman, named Jacks, belonging to a seining party, got a "jigger" into his right foot. This is a small sand-tick, or flea, whose work is as swift as, and far more deadly than, the mosquito's. When a nigger gets a "jigger" into his foot he immediately cuts out the stung part with his knife. I've seen them do it often.

Jacks didn't know what had got him at the time. He thought it was just the prong of a crab or something, and bothered no more about it. But during the night he woke us all up with his howls. Poor Jacks was in great agony, and his foot was swollen terribly.

Bunthorne, the sick-bay steward, brought the doctor, who applied fomentations and poultices, and lanced the foot; but it was no good: the thing festered and tortured the poor soul for months, the doctor tending and nursing him all the time like a mother.

One afternoon we took him ashore for a breath of land air, "chaired him" up the beach a bit, and sat him on a stone with our jumpers under him.

While we were sitting, along came the funniest-looking specimen of a native we had ever seen. He had nothing on but a loin cloth. A broken clay pipe was stuck through one of his ears, the other held a long porcupine quill. A bone ring hung from his nose, and above it was suspended a pair of spectacles, with one of the glasses broken, that must have been made when these useful contrivances were first invented. His woolly head was also stuck full of feathers from different birds. I've seen a better-looking face on an ape many a time. And yet harmlessness and good fellowship beamed from it.

He hailed us in native English, and came over *salaaming*. Seeing us smoking, he whipped out his pipe and begged a fill. When he had it going like a blast furnace he twisted himself down on the ground beside us and asked what was the matter with our chum. On being told he sprang up tapping his breast and shouting—

"Oh! me! . . . Me med'cine man! . . . Oh, yass! . . . Me cure heem! Me make heem good. . . . Oh, yass!"

Down he flopped in front of Jacks again, smelled the foot all over and then, holding up his forefinger, said Jigga!"

We all nodded "Yes," and Jacks said, looking at him admiringly, "By gum, that boy knows something!"

Up jumped Johnny. "Ah," he cried; "me know! . . . Yass . . . Jigga. Um-m! . . . Me cure heem! Yas-s!"

He wanted us to remove the bandages and let him see Jacks's foot. But this we wouldn't do: wouldn't have dared to without the doctor's permission.

Then in his funny gibberish he asked one of us to come inland a bit with him, and as I had filled his pipe for him he seemed to select me, and I, scenting an adventure, and glad of the chance, filled it again and off we went together.

He led me into a sort of jungle of scrub and high grass, through which he went as easily as I would go aloft, but which was difficult for me, so I had to bring him up.

"Here, Johnny!" I shouted. "Not so fast. Hol' on a bit!"

Back he came running, just as a dog does when out on a ramble, stopped, smiled all over his droll face, said "A' right, sah. Me fo'get. Me hurry—cure heem"—pointing to the beach—"Oh, yass!" and started on again in front, pushing the stuff aside to help me through.

Soon we got out of this and in among trees, some with huge trunks and massive branches, some long, tapering erections with a bunch of leaves at the top like a housewife's switch; others like immense ferns, their long fronds gracefully waving in the light air, which tasted delicious here, and little flowering bushes such as we have at home, like the hawthorn and the currant, only much more gorgeously dressed.

Here Johnny began to sniff, raising his head and turning it in all directions. Then he stopped, barked out "No, no, no!" and went on a bit further; I stepping gingerly among the grass, fearing snakes. But Johnny never seemed to bother about anything.

This went on for some little time, then suddenly he stopped dead, sniffed violently. "Yash!" he cried, and ran over to a tree-bole which was standing by itself in a small clearing. It looked to me to have been felled years ago either by lightning or wind, for it was covered with moss and lichen, and the top was like a dome.

This was evidently what Johnny was on the lookout for, and proved to be a deserted beehive. He asked for my knife, which I gave him, and he set to work and in two minutes had the whole dome down in his hands. He laid it tenderly on the grass, bottom up, and while I stood admiring the glistening sweet-smelling stuff, already beginning to ooze from its sides, like syrup—tasting like it, too; and, by Jingo, wasn't it rich!—Johnny himself went and brought a leaf almost as big as a lady's umbrella, and into this he scraped what honey and comb was left in the trunk—pretty nearly as much as what appeared to be in the hive.

The leaf he gave me, taking the hive himself, and carrying it like a baby, grunting and chuckling to himself all the way back to the beach like a happy old scientist who has made a "find."

We hadn't been gone half an hour altogether, but Jacks had wearied sitting, and was back in the boat again waiting for us. The cox'n (coxswain), an A.B. called Darby Kelly, first thought of taking the honey and leaving the native behind: but the poor soul looked so crestfallen at this, and seemed so interested in Jacks 's foot, and so confident of curing it, that Darby at last decided to take him with us and hear what the doctor said. So Johnny and I tumbled in, the umbrella was opened, and all of us had a good lick of the honey; the native, with the hive on his knees, holding up his hands cautioning us to be careful.

Lord! these doctors are all the same. Savage or civilized, all the world over. Forever keeping you away from what you like best.

Just as we reached the ship, Billy, who was walking in the waist, chanced to look through the gun-port, and started when he saw who was in the boat. But before he could speak, even before we had got hooked on properly, Johnny was over the side, hive and all, like a monkey, screeching to him as he had to us ashore, "Me! . . . Medicine man. . . . Tribe docta. . . . Oh yass. . . . Cure heem—yass—queek!"

This set us all a-grin, except Darby, who was responsible for the boat. Billy was a queer fish to handle, and there was no saying what he might do if he took Johnny's visit as a breach of discipline. So Darby frowned heavily, growling: "My God, I'm afraid I'm in for a row over this trip. You fellows'll have to stand by me."

By the time, however, we had got Jacks aboard and the boat hoisted, our own doctor was on deck, and he and Johnny were holding a "consultation," while Billy leaned against the bulwarks looking on.

The doctor was sitting on the wardroom hatch, with his legs spread out, and an amused, interested expression on his face, calmly regarding the native, who bounced about in front of him pointing, now to the hive and the big leaf, which lay alongside him, now to his own foot and the doctor's alternately, making motions of applying a poultice and bandage, screeching all the time: "Me! . . . Ohyass! . . . Cureheem! . . . Tribe docta. . . . Ohyass!"

The doctor, dressed in his snowy white drill, with his fine, intellectual face and manly figure, looking the very picture of civilized dignity and neatness, and Johnny, with his pipe stuck in his ear and all his other accoutrements, dancing in front of him like a living scarecrow, made a contrast that filled your heart with pity—at least it did mine. I often think that some horrible calamity will overtake the whole white race yet for the way they have murdered, robbed and taken advantage of the black, who are just as good as they are.

However, there was no fear of Johnny meeting anything but good aboard the *Swallow*. In a little while, the doctor and he—Johnny carrying the big leaf, with Bunthorne behind bringing cloths and stuff—came for'ard and gathered round the patient's cot under the fo'c'sle. Five minutes later, Jacks let out one yell, which might have reached the ears of people in England, and we heard the shrill screams of Johnny: "No, no! . . . He good! ... No hurt! A' right! . . . Oh yass!" mingled with the soothing tones of the doctor. In ten minutes more, Jacks was sound asleep.

The doctor gave orders that he wasn't to be disturbed, and went aft with Bunthorne and the leaf. We brought Johnny below, and it being tea time, and the ship's steward as much interested as the rest of us, a meal was set before him that I'll back he hadn't tasted the like of for many a day. In the middle of it, Bunthorne arrived with a big tot of grog with the doctor's compliments, so Johnny was in the Seventh Heaven.

It was amusing to see him squatting native-fashion on the lockers, beaming on everything and everybody, while the fellows hunted about for odd pieces of clothes, bits of tobacco and other things to give him.

By the time he was ready to leave we had him dressed in a bit of every rig forward: A flannel and check shirt from Dolly Brown, a pair of Darby Kelly's trousers, the steward's waistcoat, one of Bunthorne's jackets, and the bos'un's cap.

He had, besides, a bundle as big as a packman's wrapped in a piece of sail-cloth. In it were a great quantity of tobacco, a dozen or so of new clay pipes, some wooden ones, a couple of bars of soap—I remember the cook handing them down through the booby-hatch—and any number of other useful odds and ends. Altogether Johnny was pretty well set up.

But, to crown all, he took away a thing that gave him special delight. This was a mouth organ—the pet, particular enjoyment of Sharkie Bradford. Johnny took a terrible notion of it, and Sharkie, like a man, handed it over. The little man's eyes fairly glowed when he got it, and the look on his face when he put it to his mouth and blew into it, nearly drove us all into fits laughing.

Before he left the fo'c'sle he stole over and had a look at Jacks, who lay as calm as a baby, sleeping as he hadn't done for months, poor chap. "Oh, yass!" he whispered, looking funnier than ever in his new fit-out—like a pantomime pirate—"Oh, yass! . . . He good! . . . A' right!"

His fame had reached the cabin, and when the fellows came aft to see him over the side, there was the captain and all the officers waiting under the break of the poop. The doctor introduced him all round, then presented him with a purse and money which had been subscribed among them. Then the skipper and the doctor shook hands with him again, and into the boat he tumbled, surely the happiest little man in the wide continent of Africa, although the tears were running down his face like rain. And we were all as pleased as himself, I'm sure.

But he was like a child, who is elated or cast down by what the moment brings. He happened to put his hand in his pocket and felt the mouth organ. Out it came and he played and chattered to us all the way to the landing-place.

We helped him ashore with his bundle, saw him shoulder it, heard his parting scream as he broke into the jungle, and that was the last of him.

It seemed that we had entertained an angel unawares, for in two or three weeks Jacks's foot was as sound and well as any in the ship, and Bunthorne told me afterwards that the doctor held a high opinion of Johnny's skill as a medicine man, and thought Providence must have sent him.

What became of the hive I really don't remember. I think it was emptied, cleaned out, sealed up again and sent home as a curio, but I'm not sure.

Anyway it was a fine afternoon's adventure, and as such I always look back on it.

CHAPTER 18

Strange Sights Abroad

Parading up and down the coast we met many adventures and saw many strange sights.

Once we attended the crowning of a native queen and a native wedding both on the same day. The coronation took place in the afternoon, and here we had the luck to see an interesting ceremony, followed by a kind of sports—spear-throwing, wrestling, juggling, and so forth—finishing up with a feast, where the natives ate so much that they lay about like dead men, with their stomachs swollen like balloons.

The wedding was in the evening, just after sunset, and here we saw a sight which, could it be seen in London, say, would drive the population crazy—the girls anyway. This was a procession of bridesmaids.

The girls were covered with fireflies. The little glittering beetles, strung like beads, were twined round their arms, their legs, their heads and their bodies—thousands of them, falling about them, whirling around them as they walked, like cascades of fire; draping them, as it were, like Indian bead screens. You never saw a prettier sight, nor a more dainty touch given to a wedding. I thought to myself: "By Jove! Even the biggest of your millionaires couldn't beat that!"

Elephant Bay was one of our most popular places of call. The bay takes a wide sweep and swarms with fish right up to the beach, so that fine sport with the seine can be had. The sand is soft and white, the water pure and clear as the Mediterranean, and shoals so gently that the beach is made an ideal place for bathing without much fear of sharks, although, of course, you must always keep your weather eye open in case the fin of one of these pirates shows up unexpectedly. The only danger was the "Jigger" I told you about in the last chapter.

The land extends in a flat semicircle for a good distance before it meets the hills, which form an amphitheatre right round, and ends in a big bluff, cut sheer as though a knife had done it. On the face of the bluff was printed in immense letters, so as to be easily read from the anchorage, the names of the ships on the station. Of course *Swallow* was added to the list.

A long stair called "Jacob's Ladder"—I forget how many steps were in it, although we had them all counted—led to the top of the cliff. Many a time did I climb that ladder, and the view well repaid the labour. The country was thickly wooded, and there was a big pool covering a good many acres just below a particular spot where we usually halted for a smoke and a look round.

Here the animals of the wild came to drink. Often we saw a lion stalk down in his lordly fashion, quench his thirst, give out a bellow that seemed to shake the hills, and then amble off again. Sometimes a jackal would slink into view and disappear as suddenly as he came. His whine was for all the world like the cry of a baby.

Apes and monkeys galore were there. Once we got a fine sight of a gorilla—a big, massive fellow he was, with limbs like tree-branches and a proper savage-looking head.

He didn't see us, God be thanked.

Once a large herd of zebras came down. Dainty creatures they were: their striped bodies—white, yellow, brown and black—looking beautiful against the green background. They are extraordinarily quick of hearing. One of our fellows, hundreds of feet above them, started to whistle and—hanged if the whole tribe didn't disappear like a puff of smoke.

But the incident that has riveted Elephant Bay on my mind, apart from Johnny the medicine man, was one that happened in connection with a great crowd of elephants which came one evening to drink and wash their *piccaninnies*.

There must have been nearly a hundred of them. They came in a long procession through a ravine-like opening in the hill about a quarter of a mile from where we were sitting directly above the pool, so that we had a grand view of them.

Great cow and bull elephants, with long, waving trunks, and immense tusks, some straight, some bent, some almost curled. The little ones—there would be twenty of them—not much bigger than donkeys, trotted beside their mothers, or skipped about uttering little barks of pleasure, flapping their ears and frisking around and under the bodies of their elders in the manner of young things everywhere.

Sometimes a big bull would take a playful turn, seize a youngster round the middle with his trunk, hold him high aloft, and go capering about, the youngster screaming with delight and the old man chuckling just as human fathers do with their babies.

They all made for the pool: but into it the kiddies had to be driven—by force. They didn't want to be washed. When they were all in, a scene began that "beggars description," as these big writing fellows say. Such a splashing and commotion! The pool, a moment before like a silver mirror, with everything around reflected in it, now frothing like a huge cauldron of beer, and exactly the same colour. Great black trunks waving in the mist and squirting like firemen's hoses. Big bodies, little bodies, all black and shining, appearing for an instant above the water, then sinking under it. You would see a big trunk suddenly emerge grasping a little kicking body from which the water was streaming in showers, whirl in the air, and then come down, and a mighty splash would follow that "made the welkin ring." When a little one would show signs of bolting, Pa or Ma would grab the runaway, jerk him back, and in he would flounder again. Never did I see anything more interesting or exciting through the whole commission, and yet one of the fellows had to go and spoil it.

He was an ordinary seaman called Smifkin, with a mind almost as stupid as his name. He had been sitting beside a huge boulder that was slack in the earth. He kept working at it with his knife, missing all the fine show, till he got it loosed altogether. Then he sent it hurling down the hillside. It bounded from the hill and fell with a tremendous splash a short distance from where the elephants were disporting themselves, sending a column of water about twenty feet high into the air.

The effect of this was like an earthquake. There was a general stampede. The elephants seized their young, took to their heels, and through that pool into the forest they went, trumpeting and roaring and smashing everything in their way, as if Old Nick were after them. When called to account for this brain wave of his, Smifkin said he had done it for a joke!" Bumpkin" is what they should have called him.

Our Pets: Jacko

St. Paul de Loanda was another port at which we often dropped anchor and spent a good deal of time. Here we shipped Jacko, a chimpanzee, who became famous all over the station as "The *Swallow's* monkey."

He was successor to another we had earlier, called Jenny, a little toy monkey. A terrible fate overtook her. She got wet one night in the first watch, and somebody put her into the galley-oven to dry, the fire being out. But somebody else came along who didn't know she was there, and shut the oven door. In the morning Jenny was found baked to a cinder.

Jacko was "a'body's body," as we say in Scotland, meaning a universal favourite. He slept with a different man every night; and never a word was said when he was found coiled up in a hammock. The owner knew it was his turn, and just pushed him over a bit and turned in.

But, by and by we had to object, on account of his fleas. We were almost eaten alive! So we made him a snug little hammock of his own, swung it between the ventilators before the galley, provided him with a nightcap and a suit of pyjamas, and there he lay like a prince.

He very soon came to be regarded as one of the ship's company. He was allowed his tot of grog. The armourer made him a little measure like a thimble, with a tiny lug to hold it by. With this he would gravely present himself at the grog tub every day when the bugle sounded, and nod to the steward when he got it. Then he would spring on to the fore-hatch—never spilling a drop!—toss off his allowance "like a man," skip back to the fo'c'sle and replace his mug on the little shelf above his hammock, feeling that the great ceremony of the day was over.

Umbray, the ship's cook, and he became great friends. If anybody wanted the monkey Umbray was the man to tell where to find him. The two were inseparable.

Another great friend of Jacko's was Nelly, the captain's dog, a small brown spaniel. Jacko would wait patiently on the poop-ladder for her coming out of the cabin of a morning, jump on her back whenever she appeared, take her by the ears, and away the pair would go, making the deck into a racecourse.

Jacko had the run of the ship. Fore and aft, aloft or below, engine-room or stokehole—he was welcome everywhere. He was such an affectionate little soul, and would lie in your arms and grin up in your face murmuring so lovingly in his monkey lingo that you had to respond and cuddle him.

To tell all the tricks that pet of ours was up to would take a whole book to itself. One evening, while the officers were at dinner, he sprang through the wardroom hatchway, swung himself on a brass bar which crossed the centre of it, and dropped right into the soup tureen.

CRUISE OF
H.M.S. "SWALLOW"
FROM
MAY 20TH 1877
TO
MAY 20TH 1881
DISTANCE COVERED – 60,000 MILES.

I was at the wheel at the time and the hatch was just behind me. I heard the row, and when I turned and saw Jacko flash up through the hatch again covered with pea-soup, I nearly dropped the wheel laughing. He hid himself for two days after that.

Another happened after leaving Fernando Po. We came here to take in coal bricks. The negroes, standing in a long line stretching from the depot right down to our coal bunkers, passed the bricks along one by one in a continuous stream till the ship was full, which was done in no time and without the least dust or bother. Well, one night after leaving this place, Jacko abstracted a bottle of "Squaro" (Hollands Gin) from Sam Winter's locker, took out the cork, which was under a capsule—how he did it nobody could understand—and drank about a nip of the raw spirit.

Sam had the first watch that night. When he came below at eight bells and went to his locker, behold! the bottle was gone. Sam, naturally, was in a towering passion; but he had to be careful and not complain too loud as the liquor had been smuggled aboard.

I heard him curse deeply, saying "He was no man that took it, anyway, the low down . . . ." etc.

In the middle watch, after we had gone round the capstan, we were all gathered about the galley smoking and discussing Sam's loss, when the groans of somebody retching, as if sick, were heard.

"I'll bet that explains it!" said old Neddy sharply, taking the cook's lantern; "come on!" We followed the direction of the sounds and there, just abaft the funnel, holding on to a biscuit-case, while heaving as if he would turn himself inside out, was Jacko, as drunk as a lord, with the bottle between his feet.

That escapade cost him a whole week's illness, with the doctor attending him. But the great point of this story is that when he got well he wouldn't look at grog any more. If anyone offered him a drop he would spit and show his teeth. I often thought that some of us might have taken a lesson from him.

Jacko's lapse was put down to an extra turn at the grog-tub that day, and so Sam escaped suspicion. When he got his bottle back, with only the nip out of it the monkey had swallowed, he whispered gleefully: "Didn't I say he was *no man* that took it, eh?"

Skippo

Another great pet we had, and a useful one, too, was a mongoose we called Skippo, an animal like a big rat, with short legs and a long tail. But couldn't he run!—flash is more the word. He darted here and there like lightning, his eyes like pin points, and uttering sharp little sounds like "click, click."

Before we got him, the lower deck absolutely swarmed with cockroaches—long, brown, shiny insects as big as black beetles. They got into your ears; between weevils in the biscuit—we were a good few months in commission before the biscuit-tin was invented—and cockroaches in the general food; we had a lively time of it for a while. Your clothes locker was full of them, so was the bread barge.

They dropped from the beams flop into your basin or plate while you sat at meals, and this happened so often that you came to think nothing about it—just fished them out and left them wriggling on the table. If they made to run away, you just brought your spoon down whack upon them and went on with your dinner.

I am sure we must have eaten hundreds of them in the dark. It was nothing unusual for a man to spring up and howl—"Oh, Lord; I've swallowed a cockroach!" and somebody else to cry: "Give the poor thing a drink!"

They got so plentiful that we used to count our catches at every meal. A man would have six or seven ranged along the rim of his plate and would say: "There's my little bag for this adventure." I don't remember them as doing much harm, but they were a terrible pest. It was awful to feel one crawl over your face while you lay tucked in your hammock. You couldn't be bothered taking your arms out, so you just jerked him off, squashed him against your hammock-cloth, and went to sleep.

Skippo, however, altered all this. Providence had implanted in him a fine taste for cockroaches and a glorious appetite. Before he was a month aboard he had the ship comfortable again. You heard his joyful "click" everywhere. If you smelt the vermin in your locker—for they left a heavy odour behind them—you called "Skip, Skip!" and in the little fellow would glide, burrow among your clothes, and in ten minutes there wasn't a brown-back to be seen.

He also cleared the bilges of rats, and Tanky, the captain of the hold, loved him for his services, and made a particular chum of him, just as Umbray did of the monkey. It was the same with our hammocks. When Skippo passed the night with you, Mr. Cockroach was reduced to nil in the morning. Skippo was with us a long time, but one bitter night at the Falklands he died. The cold was too much for him.

We had a good number of pets; chameleons, lizards, cardinal-birds, parrots and what not. But the sweetest of all was a young gazelle which Bob Wilson bought from a black trapper in Loanda Bay.

You never saw a daintier little creature. She had a slight, lithesome, fawn-coloured body, and long tapering legs. Her horns, just beginning to sprout, looked like little mounds on the top of her pretty head. Her large, soft brown eyes were

As liquid as stars in a pool,

as Tom Hood says, and as gentle as a young maid's.

We had her about six months, but (like her famous sister) just when she came to know everybody she took distemper, through the lack of greenstuff, and though the doctor did all a man could for her, she died.

I couldn't tell you how grieved we all were over the loss of this little pet. Even the *Kroomen* were sad about it. I remember the incident of the gazelle's death particularly on account of an adventure we met with on the very day we buried poor Fanny—that was her name.

Chapter 19

The Slave Chase

We were heading for St. Paul de Loanda at the time, and Mr. Hopkins, the British Consul, was aboard. In the afternoon we sighted a brig which looked so suspicious that the captain determined to watch her. She was making for the land.

The news went through the ship that she was a slaver, and certainly when she came nearer she had all the appearance of one. A long, sinister-looking craft, with tall, tapering masts, raked aft, and covered with canvas. The telescope revealed crowds of black people aboard her.

We got steam up, took in sail, altered our rig by housing topmasts, shortening jibboom and such like manoeuvres, and passed her flying the American colours. She was a Portuguese brig, named the *Pensamento*. Her deck was full of black, woolly heads, which bobbed over the rail from every part of her.

We went by, taking no notice beyond the usual dip of the flag, then slipped into a little cove where the land was a trifle lower than our mastheads, rigged up a crow's nest on the main-royal mast, and there we lay, with a man on the lookout day and night, watching her. Two nights she kept us there in a fever of impatience; then on the evening of the third day, just after sunset, the lookout man reported her out under full sail.

Then the fun began! Down came the crow's nest, up went the sail—stun'sails, stay sails, trysails—everything that could draw, and off we went after her what we could pelt.

A fine spanking breeze from the land sent us along in grand style. At first we couldn't see the brig, but when the moon gained her splendour and turned the sea into a glory of molten silver, *then* we saw her—although not so much her in reality as the black velvety shadow she threw on the glittering surface over which she went like an ominous bird.

My word, couldn't she sail! Bending over so that sometimes we could have seen her bilge-boards had we been nearer, she simply flew over the water. Her people had seen us, knew that we were after them; guessed, I daresay, our stratagem of three days ago; and the Portugee skipper, knowing the qualities of the little vessel under him, and confident of out-sailing us before morning, determined to pull us after him—give us a nice little outing, in fact, and himself the joy of beating a "Johnny Anglesh, damn him!" and tell his cronies all about it when he got into port.

Well, sport is dear to the British heart, and as it was a fine night we had no objections. But, I tell you, the excitement aboard our hooker was something to keep the blood warm. Our fellows danced about the deck rubbing their hands and chuckling "Go it old bird! After her! Fetch her in, little girl!"

But it was soon seen, that the *Swallow* was no match for the *Pensamento*—not in that wind, anyway. She easily went one and a half knots to our one. She bounded over the silver wavelets like a thing of life, clothing herself in glittering sparks from her forefoot, like the girls in the African village with their fireflies, leaving a wake behind her like the steam of a railway train; and seeming to laugh at our efforts to catch up with her.

We admired that little brig. Admired, too, the fine sailorly way she was handled, but we meant to have her all the same, ay, if we sailed to hell after her to do it.

Steam was up, so the push of the screws was added to the sails, and now the little *Swallow's* heart began to beat in earnest. We looked over the side to see the effect, but there wasn't much difference; she seemed to be almost doing her utmost under the pressure of canvas. But she dipped her beak in the wave, bent over to the race, flicking the spray as high as the fore-yard, and sending her wake boiling away astern like the wash of a river over rocks, and behaving as lively as her nimble namesake.

But it was no use. The brig gradually edged away.

A shot from the 7-inch gun was sent after her. Her skipper answered this by setting his stun'sails. Another, a little nearer this time. A loud shout of laughter, which went from the fo'c'sle to the poop, where the officers were all gathered watching the brig with their glasses, followed this second messenger.

We could still make out objects on the brig, and distinctly saw her skipper jump on to the taffrail, his figure twinkling under the glowing moon like a mannikin, smack his breech energetically and twiddle his fingers at us in contempt, twisting himself side-on to let us see him do it.

"By God, he's a plucky one!" somebody bawled. "But we'll have you yet, you ruddy old pirate!"

Another laugh greeted this prophecy, with a note of derision in it, however, for on the face of it it looked silly to hope for anything of the kind. And yet it worked out all right as events turned, proving the truth of Scott's remark about the shaft at random sent.

Meantime, the additional thrust of her stun'sails put more life into the brig than ever, and she began to leave us hand over fist—melt away, in fact, before our eyes—till by and by all we could make out was a glittering pin-point on the horizon.

We thought we had lost her, and were cursing our rotten luck and calling the ship bad names, when suddenly the wind lulled and hope revived. Feverishly we took in the stun'sails, trimmed the yards to catch every breath—for it had changed a little—and after her we flew, saying our prayers again like true sailors.

The way we lifted the brig now showed that she had hardly any wind at all. We overhauled her as an express does a goods train. Soon she began to show up; then to take shape; then we could distinguish her individual sails; then out popped her black hull, and she lay broad to view just as we had seen her at first.

Our fellows went dancing mad about the t'-gallant fo'c'sle, shaking hands and telling each other about the prize-money that would line our handkerchiefs by and by, crying "Good little girlie!" "Pretty little swallow-tail!" "Catch her, pussy; there's the mouse ahead, dear!" and Buntin, whose watch below it was, began to carol:

When the swallows homeward fly.

Oh, we were the happy crowd!

Aft on the poop the officers were just as excited as ourselves, although, of course, they wouldn't show it. They never do, these people. Their dignity won't allow them. They stand as glum as undertakers, even on the most whirling occasions, and yet they must have their happy moments like the rest of us.

Our boys aft tried to make believe they took this business all in the day's work. But their manners betrayed them. The way they fussed with their glasses, clapt them to their eyes, took them away again, and fidgeted about the deck, showed that the blood was running as warm aft as it was forward. Routh, I'm sure, would be boiling. He was a rare sport. The captain, with his cap "on three hairs," as they say at sea, meaning stuck right on the back of his head (a sure sign that he was pleased), was standing beside Mr. Hopkins, sending his glances everywhere at once—at the sky, the sails, the brig ahead, the smoke pouring from the funnel—everywhere at the same time, and all the time as dignified as a bishop.

Mr. Hopkins himself, a terribly grave gentleman on duty, though an irresistible comic when off, stood on the poop as straight as a pole, with his hands behind his back, and his fingers twitching as if he would give the world to have them at somebody's throat. And the gleam of the chase in their eyes they couldn't hide, not they! Westwater, who was signalman on duty at the time, told me afterwards that he would gladly have forfeited his grog for a whole week just for the privilege of letting out one yell. That'll tell you how things were aft.

All this time the moon was flooding the sea with silver light. Soon we came up to within a mile of the brig, and then we saw three hangdog, miserable-looking figures standing aft by the helm. The skipper himself—a proper-looking sea-jackal he!—with his ugly head crammed into a Mexican hat—stumping athwartships in front of them like a pendulum.

The first cutter was ordered away, and as this was the boat I belonged to, I was in her waiting to be lowered. She hung on the starboard quarter, and as the brig was to starboard of us, I had a good view of the proceedings.

Everything was ready; the crew lined up in the gangway; Mr. Hopkins, in his ordinary wearing clothes, the first lieutenant and the paymaster, the former wearing his sword-belt, standing by to go with us when—hanged if the wind didn't freshen again and off went the brig!

You should have seen the stampede aboard of that little hooker! Her people sprang into life as if somebody had set fire to them. Up went the stun'-sails, which had been taken in. A sharp shower came on, just heavy enough to soak the sails and give them a better draw—as if to help her, you would have thought!—and away she went like a racehorse.

It was like snatching a bone from a dog! If you had heard the remarks on the *Swallow*, you would have thought sailors a rum lot—which they are, really.

121

However, it was only an expiring puff. It didn't carry us more than two miles, although the brig did about four, when it dropped altogether and went dead calm.

Then the hallelujahs started again!

"Hands furl sail!" "Down! gallant yards!" "Loose fore and main trysails!" etc.

In half an hour we were lying within a couple of cable-lengths of her, on a sea like a lady's mirror, just dimmed occasionally by the clouds crossing the moon, as her breathing does when she brings the glass too close. In five minutes more the boat was in the water, and, with the three officers in the stern, was making towards her in fine style.

(I have a picture hanging in front of me while I write which shows this part of the proceedings and recalls the incident vividly. It was drawn by Buntin and reproduced in the illustrated papers of that year.)

We smelt the brig as we came nearer. By the time the bowman got hooked on alongside we felt almost suffocated. What a stench! The paymaster, who was a delicate-looking young gentleman, had his handkerchief to his nose as he crossed the gangway, and whenever the three left the boat we dropped astern a bit to get away from it. One of the fellows remarked: "It'll take a lot of prize-money beer to wash this down, hearties!" I never came across a smell like yon in all *my* life.

The Portuguese captain, a swarthy, beetle-browed ruffian, with two other yellow-faced beauties—his mates, I daresay—was waiting for us, and there were a good few more lowering heads sprinkled along the port bulwarks. As our officers stepped aboard we heard the skipper say in a gruff voice: "*Veil*, vat you want? Vat you mean by intervereing *mit* mee? Firing shotts at mee—on *de* high seeass! By *Gott*, you catch it for dis!"

Then we dropped out of earshot. There seemed to be any quantity of blacks aboard, judging from the woolly heads that kept popping up and disappearing from every quarter. Big heads, little heads, some of them belonging to girls by the look of them, some to mere children, all black as soot and staring at us with big, wistful eyes.

The officers were gone only about a quarter of an hour when back came Billy and beckoned us alongside again. As they got into the boat we saw by the grinning faces of the Portugee and his mates that all our hopes of prize-money had gone by the board.

Mr. Richmond, the paymaster, with his handkerchief still at his nose, implored us to put our backs into the oars; to get away from that floating cesspool as quick as ever we could. But he needn't have minded; we were just as eager to get away as he was. The three officers conversed together while we rowed back, but all I heard (for I was pulling second bow), was part of a remark by Mr. Hopkins about "caution being very necessary in affairs of that kind."

However, when we got the boat hoisted, and dropped aboard again, the ship's head was turned towards St. Paul de Loanda, and the brig left a good couple of miles astern.

Then we heard the result. It seemed that although there were over 700 negroes—men, women and children—on board that brig, we couldn't touch her skipper because he had papers certifying every one of them to be labourers going to South America to be employed in the rice and cotton fields. Not a manacle nor an iron was aboard of her—I believe they got rid of these things during the last lap of the chase. She was a slaver all right, only the brutes that commanded her were too cute to let themselves be caught.

Anyway, they got clear. It was a terrible disappointment to us; and it took the splicing of the main brace and a sing-song under the glorious moon to cheer the way back to port, and make up for it.

Then, after St. Paul, Ascension was our next stop and, after that, St. Helena, and a long kick of the heels ashore, so there was balm ahead!

CHAPTER 20

"Lady" Johnson's Dream

St. Helena was the favourite port on the station. We had general leave here—sometimes a week—seven whole days, when you could have your chum along with you and go rambling over the island at your own sweet will, and free from all naval restraint. That was the prime feature of it! Here we lost a messmate of mine who was very popular in the ship.

A queer fate was his. This was the boy who had been nicknamed Spooney on account of the Southsea Common affair (by the way, it was his sister he had been sitting with that afternoon), then Molasses, after falling into the barrel of treacle, and finally Lady, because of the lovely "girl" he made in our dramatic representations—he and West-water, the signalman, sustaining the female parts.

Johnson was a fine-looking lad. Tall, with dark brown, crinkly hair, big luminous eyes, the high nose of the aristocrat, and the air of a young lord. His appearance suggested a better walk of life than that from which the common Jack is usually drawn: not from any presuming on his part, but just—you know what I mean—that indefinable "something" that marks "the swell."

He, Jack Belton and I, the three boys of the mess—all rated "men" now, of course—were good chums. Johnson was "dinghy boy," but not the one who brought me from the Duke to the Swallow.

When I said that we had only one death aboard during the commission, I meant, of course, by sickness. This was a different thing altogether; and the circumstances leading up to the final act of the tragedy, for tragedy it was, were so strange, that I shouldn't wonder if you doubt my word when I tell you about them. If you do, well, I must just refer you to that oft-repeated observation addressed by Hamlet to Horatio, and go on with my story.

Well, the curtain was rung up one Thursday afternoon when we were leaving Ascension Island to catch the mail-boat from England, previous to making our call at St. Helena.

We were under steam, and Thursday being make-and-mend-clothes day, the deck was pretty lively. Some of the fellows were sewing, others netting window-curtains, making daisy mats, or pictures worked in wool upon stretched canvas—Darby Kelly had one finished of a ship in full sail which you could hardly have told at a distance from an oil painting—some writing letters home, and all chatting away meanwhile.

A few, among whom was Lucks with his concertina, were under the fo'c'sle. One was singing a version of "Ben Block's Cap," and the chorus:

In the Med-it-ter-a-a-nee-an!
In the Med-it-ter-a-a-nee-an!
I'm going home, for I've lost my lo-o-ove,
In the Med-it-ter-a-a-nee-an!

came down to us and was taken up with great gusto and sent rolling on deck again.

It was wet on deck, and what little air there was, was sultry and heavy. The scuttles were open, and I was standing on my locker looking at the land, which lay on our port beam and loomed in the dim light like a huge cinder, and watching the sea squirting up through the blow-holes like spouts from a whale-school, when a sudden hush behind caused me to turn round.

Johnson was leaning against a ventilator and all hands had stopped what they were at and were looking at him. Mick Leonard, our prize Banshee story-teller, was lying on the gunner's-chest amidships with his hands supporting his chin, and on him Johnson had his eyes earnestly fixed as if expecting him to say something.

Mick was a rough-looking chap, whose two upper incisors stuck the lip out and gave his face a ferocious turn. But he had no more harm in him than an Irish terrier. His was the pure Hibernian cast of countenance: snub nose, long upper lip, and the expression of humour and cordiality so characteristic of Erin's sons. He had also a rich, round brogue. As a sailor-man Mick was nowhere, but at a good Irish ditty, or the telling of a blood-curdling yarn, few could equal him.

Presently he said (you can think you hear the brogue; I know I couldn't reproduce it, so I won't try). "Well, Lady, that's the queerest drame entirely. Let's hear it again."

I could easily see that something extra special had been going on which I had lost. I slipped down and sat on the locker.

"What's up?" I asked, looking around. "Lady; what's it all about?"

"Oh, nothing," Johnson answered; "Just a dream I had last night that I was telling Mick."

"An' a funny drame, too," said Mick.

"Well, what's it about?—Did you hear?" I asked Dolly Brown, who was sitting next me sewing a new seat into his serge trousers.

"Bits," Dolly replied. "But I can't make head or tail of it—Spin it over again, Lady. Mick's a good reader of dreams; a regular Joseph he is, he'll put you right. Come on."

"Oh, do Lady!" I cried, my curiosity bubbling up, and scenting a good thing from the way Mick was looking at my chum. "Come on, butty; let's hear it." (Had I known what was coming, I'm very sure I shouldn't have been so eager!)

The others chimed in: "That's right." "Spin away Lady." "We're all a-listenin'."

Johnson shifted his position, and his fine eyes wandered over the crowd. "Oh," he said, "it's hardly worthwhile. It's only a dream and there's nothing in it. However, as you will have it, it was this way:

"I thought we were lying at St. Helena, and the dinghy was called away to fetch somebody from the shore. It was evening. There was no wind, but a choppy sea was on; and I remember I wondered at that. When I was about a hundred yards from the landing-place I heard the rollers bashing against the rocks and knew it would be a bit rough getting in. I took a glance round to make sure of my direction, and just then "caught a crab" with the port oar which upset me. Before I could right myself a wave came and knocked the oar out of my hand, and carried it away.

"I shipped the remaining oar in the stern rowlock and sculled about looking for the other, but darkness came down suddenly and I could not see it. I was just making up my mind to scull back to the ship when another wave struck the dinghy, pitched me on my back right under the th'art, and unshipped the only oar I had left.

"Then I thought the darkness got quite black; the boat drifted out to sea, and—I don't know what happened afterwards, but I woke shivering all over."

A long pause followed.

"What had you for your dinner yesterday, Lady?" cried Bill Grimshaw, a jolly-faced, red-whiskered leading stoker from the mess next to ours.

"Pork and pea-soup: same as yourself," said Johnson, smiling.

"Doughboy?" said Bill, with his eye cocked.

Johnson nodded.

"Ah, then," said Grimshaw, in a tone of conviction; "that accounts for it. You must blame old Slushy."

"That be blowed for a yarn!" exclaimed a voice from the booby hatch overhead, where the cook was peering down as eager as the rest of us, "Slushy has nothing to do with it."

"Away and clean your greasy coppers out!" cried Bill.

"Why, you bloomin' ginger-headed, swab-faced, shovel-engineer, what do you know about dreams or doughboys either?" cried the cook, who was a Westcountryman, and ready for a growl with anybody on the shortest notice, "Coal dust is all you know about."

"Order, please, in the galley!" sang out Neddy Pearce, from the other side of the deck. "Hol' on, my hearties, and let's hear what the oracle has to say. There's something mighty peculiar about that there dream to my way of thinkin', eh, Mick?"

"Ay," said Mick, who had never altered his position, but lay staring at Johnson with his brows puckered like a bellows. "Ah; there's something mighty queer about it. Is your father and mother alive, Lady?"

"No, they're both dead."

"Have ye any relations?"

"Yes," said Johnson, his face lighting up, seemingly at the thought of them, "I've two sisters."

"Is them all the friends ye have?"

"Yes," said Johnson, fascinated by Mick's eye, "All I have in the world."

"Ah, thin," said the Irishman, in a voice that sounded like the croak of a raven, and sent a creepy sensation down my spine, "poor, poor Lady; you'll never see your sisters more!"

A shudder ran through the deck, and somebody shouted, "Cover him up!"

"Not see my sisters more," cried Johnson, his eyes filling, "what do you mean?"

Before Mick could reply, however, a squirt of tobacco-juice took him fair on the bridge of the nose, and *his* filled, though from different emotions. He rolled off the chest, and lay writhing on the deck, while a yell of laughter went up from all hands. The pain must have been dreadful, for when he got up his eyes were like a pair of over-ripe tomatoes, and gave such a ludicrous expression to his face that another yell broke out.

He glowered savagely at the grinning faces around him, and said: "Yes; laugh away, ye durty omadons! But if I knew who did that, it's a different key he would cackle in, the scurvy pock-puddin' that he is!—Wait; ye may laugh as ye like, but see if my words don't come true."

After this there was a general rush on deck for a smoke; and other things coming about, Lady's dream and Mick's interpretation were entirely forgotten.

Some days later we made the point we were steering for; met the mail-boat, and soon had the letters aboard. Immediately afterwards we started for St. Helena.

The arrival of the mail was always a momentous event in life at sea in my day. For the time being, work was practically suspended, and the men had ample leisure to discuss the news from home.

On this occasion the mail happened to be a double one, and as nearly all hands had participated, the ship was pretty happy. I remember I had two letters myself—one from my dear old mother, and one from—somebody else. These kept my mind busy with visions of one kind and another till tea-time.

During this meal, as usual after a mail, the various items of news were freely circulated and commented upon. While this was going on, somebody said: "Where's Lady?" and then it was noticed that Johnson hadn't been seen since the letters came aboard. Belton and I at once went on the hunt. We naturally went on deck first, searched the fo'c'sle, the waist, around the funnel and the 7-inch gun, then back to the fo'c'sle, again, asked the *Kroomen*, and looked everywhere, but no trace of him could we find. Then we went down below right into the fore-peak, and there we found him hidden away and crying like to break his heart.

We got him out, the other fellows gathered round, and everybody did the best he could to soothe him. The common sailor is supposed to be a rough, rowdy animal, but he can be very tender at times, as poor Johnson no doubt felt.

And really it was heartrending to look at him. His whole body shook with the violence of his sobs, and when asked to tell what had happened, he hiccupped so much that the words couldn't come out.

He threw down two letters on the mess table which Ginger

opened and read. Both were deeply edged with black. One was from his younger sister telling of the sickness and death of the elder, the other was from a friend intimating the death of the younger.

After these letters were read, especially the first, which was worded in the most tender, affectionate language, I'm safe to say there wasn't a dry eye on the lower deck.

Poor fellow. How we sympathised with him!

Most of us had someone to think of, or who would be thinking of us, at home. But here was poor Johnson left utterly alone in the world. The sad news cast a damper on the whole ship's company, who had all been so happy but a few minutes before.

Presently Mick Leonard, who belonged to No. 3 Mess on the starboard side, spoke—and again his voice sounded in my ears like the croaking of some devil-bird: "Bhoys; didn't I tell ye so!"

Lucks, one of his messmates, flung a basinful of cold tea in his face, shouting angrily, "Here, damn you! stop that biddy jargon, or I'll wring your neck for you!"

"Ye'll do less, mate, wid more ease!" shouted Mick, mopping himself with his handkerchief. "What have I done but read the drame? It's a durty skunk ye are to trate any man that way. Besides," he added significantly, edging away from Lucks, who was a much bigger man than he, "Besides, it's not all read yet. That's only the oars lost. The boat has got to go to say!"

"You Irish beast! . . ." howled Lucks, preparing to spring over the table. "By the lord Harry!" but fortunately at that moment "Evening Quarters" was sounded and everything having perforce to give way for Duty, the peace of the ship was saved.

For some days our chum was inconsolable, but gradually the raw edge of his grief wore off, and things went on in the usual routine.

By and by we reached the romantic little island, rendered famous by the imprisonment and death in one of its little farmhouses of the greatest figure in history, certainly the greatest, most feared enemy Britain ever knew.

A description of that sweet little gem of the ocean, with a sketch of its people, their manners and customs, and all the rest of it, might be very interesting here; but you'll get that in any library, far better done than I could do it, so I'll just hurry on and not break the thread of my story.

To us it was the sweetest, prettiest, balmiest little spot we touched at; at some seasons we got the scent of its geraniums far out at sea, and at all seasons a most hearty welcome. The people used to throng the landing-place when we arrived, the garrison turned out to a man— even the very flowers, we used to think, put on their best look to welcome us in. We loved to visit it.

However, for a fortnight on this, our last sojourn, all went well. Then one evening the dinghy was called away to bring an officer aboard. Johnson jumped in as usual. The weather was calm, the sea, with the exception of a slight swell, as smooth as a bowling green. There was also plenty of light for the trip, there and back. The idea of an accident happening never entered a single head. Certainly not Johnson's. He had taken the journey scores of times and, naturally, never gave it a thought.

At certain times boats, especially small boats like the dinghy, are not allowed ashore, on account of what they call "the rollers" being on. These rollers are immense waves which strike the bluff face of the island with the full force of the Atlantic, and make landing extremely difficult. This evening, however, the weather was so mild that they were overlooked.

How it happened no one knew, but just as the landing-place was reached, the boat capsized and Johnson was tossed out, flung with a merciless crash against the rocks, and immediately disappeared.

The dinghy was picked up shortly after, staved in, and with both oars gone. Nor was a sight or sign of them ever seen or heard of.

When the news was brought aboard, you can imagine the state of the lower deck. "Consternation" would just about describe it. Poor Lady's dream was discussed in whispers, and Mick's interpretation of it with bated breath. Both had come true to the very letter, as the saying is. A most uneasy, wretchedly uncomfortable feeling pervaded the ship. Sailors, as a rule, aren't the most profound philosophers, and Mick, poor soul, although he had nothing to do with it, was held in some way accountable for Johnson's death, and looked upon as a sort of Jonah who ought to be pitched overboard. I, myself, I well remember, used to look at him with awesome dread, and had he come upon me in the dark and touched me I'm sure I should have jumped into the sea. He was taken aft and questioned, but, of course, sent back again at once with nothing against him. All the same, I wouldn't have been in Mick's place—no, not for the whole year's pay of an admiral.

Nine days after, an event occurred that somewhat relieved the tension: Lady's body was recovered, battered and bruised almost beyond recognition; but it was Johnson all right. It was real! He hadn't vanished out of our ken like one of Mick Leonard's spooks. We had him with us; had him to feel, to look at—sad though the look was—and finally to tuck away in a manner becoming to a sailor who had friends left behind him. This thought brought immense comfort.

All the last sad offices to the dead—the laying of him out; sewing him up in his hammock; the making of his coffin—a labour of love to old "Chips" all the preparations for a naval funeral with full honours, were gone into with a melancholy satisfaction impossible to describe. The superstitious dread was lifted from the lower deck and everybody breathed freely again. Lucks even brought out his concertina that night, and Curly Millet sang "All's Well."

On the day of the funeral the sun shone as it can shine only in those latitudes. And certainly a more impressively solemn or imposing spectacle than the burial of our young comrade never was witnessed in St. Helena since the day it was discovered; not even the burial of Napoleon himself, so an old man told us.

The sad and strange circumstances connected with Johnson's death, and the fact of his being well known, and as well liked in the town, drew old and young, rich and poor to pay their last tribute of respect to his remains.

As the procession slowly wended its way to the cemetery, it seemed as if every man, woman and child who could possibly come was there.

When a gentle eminence a little above the town was reached, the ship, which had been his home, and wherein he had spent many a happy hour, hove into view. The peak was lowered, and the flag at half-mast swayed slowly to and fro as if waving a last farewell. As the procession passed, a funeral salute was fired, and the deep solemn boom of the guns reverberating over the sparkling surface of the sea struck each heart with a peculiar *pathos*.

At the grave, surrounded by bare-headed men and weeping women, the good old Bishop read the Service for the Dead. The beautiful words, bringing consolation and comfort to every listener, spoken in a voice that trembled with feeling—for the Bishop knew our shipmate well—were heard with the purest reverence and found an echo in every bosom.

When the service was finished a deep hush fell on the multitude, and for the first time in my life I heard the clods rattle on the coffin of somebody I loved. *That*, to me, is the most hideous and horrible of all sounds.

There is a note of finality, a suggestion of complete, thoroughly wrought out, ultimate extinction in it that numbs the brain and paralyses the heart. To me it speaks Doom—the finish of everything. The end of all—life, love, good-fellowship, kindness, goodness, sweetness, charity—the banging of the door on everything that is worth anything in this world. I hate to hear it, and would sooner go to fifty weddings than one funeral.

However, to finish my story.

Presently, the voice of the chief-gunner's mate, abrupt and sharp, broke upon the air: "Company, 'tention! Ready; present; fire!"

The last three volleys—intended, as I have heard old seamen say, to lift the departed soul into Paradise—were fired, the Last Post, his *Requiem* (poor Jack Belton, who was bugler, nearly broke down in the middle of it), was sounded: the earth quickly filled in; and, to the strains—not altogether inappropriate in this instance—of "The girl I left behind me," we marched away, leaving our shipmate to his long, last sleep in a little hollow of the hill (not unlike a hammock), encompassed on all sides by the broad waters of the Atlantic.

I was glad to get back to the ship, for a more heart-rending business I had never heard of, much less taken part in.

It was long before the impression it made on the ship's company wore away, if, which I question very much, it ever entirely did.

For one thing, although the *Swallow* was well on for two years in commission after the events here recorded, not a man of us would dare say he'd had a dream if Mick Leonard were present.

In time, however, the superstitious fear of the Irish- man gradually died down, and it was only when Lady's name was mentioned, or when Mick spun us one of his Banshee hair-raisers, that the feeling returned. As a shipmate he wasn't a bad sort at all—genial, obliging and good at a song or a yarn. Besides, as he himself said—what harm had he done?

How he managed to piece things together and foretell the future we could never find out. When asked, he said his mother could read dreams, and that he could, too, now and again. That was all we could get out of him.

Doubtless some of my readers better versed in the occult than I am will be able to throw some light on the subject. This sort of thing is taking hold nowadays. Perhaps the solution of the mystery lies in Campbell's well-known line:

Coming events cast their shadows before.

Which shadows, Mick, with his gift of second sight, was possibly able to pierce and see beyond.

Chapter 21

St. Helena

Shortly after we buried Lady, two French men-of-war, a *corvette* and a big frigate, came to the island and anchored not far from where we lay. Their officers came aboard to pay their respects to ours, and great courtesies were exchanged between them. We common Jacks found the Frenchmen splendid fellows, ready to hob-nob with us to our hearts' content.

Being better up to the "Lions" than they, we showed them around. I forget a good many of the points of St. Helena, but a few still cling to memory. One in particular was a hole in a lonely rock called "The Emperor's Eye." This was a huge mass of stone with a tunnel drilled right through as if done by a "bit" in the hand of a mighty giant. Here Napoleon was said to come often. Standing behind the hole, the effect was like looking through a telescope. Of course, you saw nothing but sky and water—limitless water—but the sea seemed bluer, and the sky-tints richer and more distant than when gazed at from the open.

It seemed, too, to make you feel your own insignificance as nothing else could—at least it did me. You felt a poor, poor atom indeed looking out on that unfathomable globe of sea and sky with nothing living breaking its serene immensity, not even a bird. I used to wonder to myself what was it brought that great spirit here so often. He who at one time held the destinies of the world in his hands. What must he have thought!

Another place of interest was the Geranium Valley, the walk to which formed one of our favourite rambles. The road, winding away from the town, rose to a peak which overhung a sort of ravine where the flowers of the geranium bloomed in such profusion that the eye was almost dazzled looking at them, while their perfume scented the island like a summer-house.

We used to say the Garden of Eden couldn't possibly have looked prettier than this. Billowing over the opposite hill, the flowers broke and fell in plumes and tufts and feathers of colour cloud. Here, trailing down the hillside in cascades of vermillion and orange; there, topping the crest of some immense boulder, overhanging and draping it in festoons of living emerald and pink, the grey tones and hues of the stone beneath gleaming palely through. Here, suspended from some jutting rock, and falling like golden stalactites in a cave, and the colour darting everywhere from their glittering facets as the light air moved them, like rays from prisms. Here a slab of soft-hued mother of pearl; there a massed battalion of red-coated soldiers; over there, look, a patch of shining snow. All the colours of the rainbow blended in exquisite harmony—a glorious poem in tone. Such loveliness you couldn't imagine. The whole scene, in fact, struck upon your sight with such impelling brilliance that your eye was momentarily blinded. I loved to come here!

One morning, shortly after sunrise, while walking towards this little paradise, we came upon a fig tree quite leafless, but with one solitary fig, about the size and shape of a Jargonelle pear, glistening on a bare branch. We plucked and ate it sitting by the roadside. A daintier morsel never passed my lips.

At first we used to have a native with us to show the particular points associated with Napoleon: the places where the sentries were posted; the limits of his wanderings; his favourite exercising ground, etc.; but we soon swallowed all he had to tell, and took the road for ourselves. When the Frenchmen came we were able to trot them around without any outside help.

Naturally, Longwood, the house where Napoleon lived and died, and another little bungalow called "The Briars," where he first put up on coming ashore, took premier place with them. Here they simply wallowed in interest—bathed in it, as it were—crossing the thresholds like pilgrims visiting The Sepulchre.

At the time it struck me as strange that men should be so filled with admiration—adoration rather— for one, who, I believed, had wrought such havoc on their country. I do not think it strange now, nor do I wonder that Napoleon's memory is cherished in the hearts of Frenchmen as it is. His personality, judging from the way the natives spoke about him, must have been very sweet.

That these French chums of ours loved their old Emperor there was no gainsaying: "Na-po-le-ong! Na-po-le-ong! Ah! . . ." they used to say, shrugging their shoulders, and raising their hands and eyes in reverential devotion.

Here is an instance I remember vividly. We had taken them to see the exile's grave. This is a square patch of grass with a railing round it, not far from Longwood. Of course *we* didn't attach much importance to it, having seen it so often, but the Frenchmen stood bowed and bareheaded, as people do in church, the picture of silent reverence, never moving a joint. One of our fellows, Tom Carter—a smart seaman, bowman of the galley he was—rather a saucy billet aboard a warship—Tom, without thinking, squirted some tobacco-juice on to the railings and the sward beyond. A Frenchman seeing this, ran at him with a shocked, pained look, crying "Oh, Johnny, Johnny, Johnny!"

Carter, who was a natty sailor, and took great pride in his appearance, immediately whipped out his handkerchief, wiped the railing, then off with his cap and polished it with that, spoiling his clean white cap-cover; whereupon the Frenchman flew at him, took him round the neck and kissed his face all over.

If you'd seen Carter during this ordeal you would have laughed!

L'Entente Cordiale

Those fellows treated us well. They got up a concert and ball in our honour. The yards were canted and the two ships moored together. The frigate was turned into a ballroom, the corvette into a supper and concert room. The Governor and other notabilities ashore, with their ladies, were invited, the weather was simply superb, and didn't we have a grand night! If ever there was an *entente cordiale* that was it!

Of course we hadn't room to return the compliment, but we made a rendezvous with them at Simon's Town, and there we engaged a large barn-like structure belonging to the Cosmopolitan Hotel, fitted it up, decorated it so that the people didn't know their own place, and had another glorious night. It was a case of

Willie brewed a peck o' maut,

and the sun was well up before the festivities terminated.

If there were more of those "jinks" there would be less danger of war, I'm thinking.

A feature of these entertainments that I particularly remember was the fun caused by the inability of the Frenchmen and ourselves to understand each other's language. We had two interpreters on our side. One was Maggar, an able seaman belonging to the Channel Islands. But he had only a smattering of French, an odd phrase or two, and, besides, he got so well sprung early in the evening at Simon's Town that he fancied he knew more than he actually did, and nearly made a mess of things. We had to put him to bed.

The other was "Gentleman George," a splendid shipmate, who afterwards turned out to be the runaway scion of a big house at home. He could speak French like a native; but as he could only be in one place at once, much of what was said was lost to the others. But the Frenchies were even worse off than we. Not one of their crowd could talk our lingo.

However, we got on all right. We just signed and kissed and cuddled each other all night.

When a French toast was given—it was toasting all the time, after supper; we toasted everything conceivable on land and water, the ladies, of course, coming top—a Frenchman would rise, glass in hand, strike an attitude, smile upon the company—taking us all in his arms, as it were—jabber out his message, George shouting the English of it after him. Then we would rise in a body, clink our glasses together, and yell at the highest pitch of our voices:

To arms! To arms, ye braves!
Avenging swords unsheath

finishing the verse as we knew how.

When it was our turn, George would get up, wave his glass aloft, return the smile, nod from side to side—George could do it like a courtier!—and say: "Gentlemen, the toast which it is my pleasant duty to propose is (so and so)," and up we would all jump, clink again, and roar:

R-r-rule Britannia! Britannia r-r-rules the waves
Br-r-ritons never-r-r, never-r-r never-r-r,—etc.

this being the only British song known to our chums—and couldn't they roll the r's!

These are two of the happiest nights I remember.

We had another with the men of the *Forester*, a sister ship on the station, and one or two with the *Dwarf*, our relief ship, and any amount of "ship-visiting" and other parties. Indeed, those junkets were frequent with us, but the best remembered are the two the Frenchmen shared.

At Simon's Town we had another glimpse of African royalty, when Cetewayo, the Zulu king and his party arrived in the s.s. *Nature, en route* for Cape Town, at the close of the war. Cetewayo was a big, massive, jolly personage, with a laugh like a thunder-roll.

The ladies of the party included three wives, one daughter and several maids of honour. They were all gorgeously dressed, but their style of beauty didn't appeal to me.

Talking about Cetewayo's ladies reminds me of a little incident which showed how keen everybody on board the *Swallow* was to see a real white face belonging to one of our own breed again. It was after leaving Simon's Town.

We were at sea, coming near Table Bay, and the weather lovely. It was my watch below, and I was sitting on my locker sewing, when an eager voice shouted through the booby hatch, "Hey, you fellows! Hurry up and see this! Quick! for heaven's sake!"

Wondering what the mischief was up, I popped my sewing into the locker and was on deck in half a minute. We were rounding a little green tongue of land that jutted into the sea like a walnut-leaf, and ended in a pretty bit of beach with a white skiff turned bottom-up on it. The land, sloping towards a house with Dutch blinds and some trees around it, was as smooth and green as a billiard table, and on a white shell walk, which stretched from the house to the beach, was a young lady slowly coming in our direction reading a book.

She had yellow hair, which fell like a waving golden cloud about her shoulders, and was dressed in white muslin or something, with a blue sash round her waist, the ends of which floated away in the breeze, and a bunch of bright red flowers pinned to her breast. I have only to shut my eyes to see her as plainly now as I did then. She looked the very living embodiment of our flag. She would be about seventeen I should think, and extraordinarily pretty she appeared to us men who had seen nothing but blacks and *yamstocks*, thick lips and flat faces, for months and months.

We were passing quite close, under sail, sliding along and making not the least noise. Everybody fore and aft was feasting his eyes on that dainty figure when, happening to raise hers, she saw us. Bang went the book, round she wheeled, and off to the house she went like a butterfly fluttering home. We called after her: "Oh! don't run away, missie! Don't run away!" She never turned nor looked back, but reached the house and vanished inside.

One of the fellows said: "Damnation" and that expressed the feelings of us all.

The whole trip to Cape Town was rotten that year. We hadn't long rounded Green Point, the place I have mentioned, and come within sight of Table Mountain, when we saw it had on its "night-cap," and before we reached the anchorage, one of the terrific squalls common to that region, came on, which nearly capsized us, blew us out to sea nearly as far as Tristan D'Acunha, and cost us a whole suit of sails.

Then, when we did get ashore two of our fellows got robbed and put into the lock-up. We had a horrible fight with some *Dagoes* in a public house, where I got a wrist sprained and a knock on the head with one of those old-fashioned ginger-beer bottles, like a torpedo.

Altogether, it was a rough time, and we were glad to get away—blaming that little gipsy at Green Point for the whole show, of course!

From then on it was nothing but gales, tornadoes and rain for nearly a month. Once, at n o'clock in the first watch (six bells) the pipe went—"Clear lower deck!" and up we bundled to find the ship almost amongst breakers. The weather was like a soldier's blanket and as thick as soup, the breakers, like mad devils, howling on our lee—couldn't we hear them! and a sou'-westerly hurricane doing its damnedest to drive us on top of them.

However, by good luck—not to mention good seamanship—and, mind you, it takes some brains, and some nerve, too, to get out of a situation like that—a night like a pocket, a roaring, tumbling sea, breakers ahead, and, a wind full of sleet and spite behind you!—but, glory be! they were both on the *Swallow's* poop that night. We managed to steer clear with never a scratch.

Then we anchored at a place called Rock Fort, a little below Cape Frio, and there we had a "Sway the main," that is, a royal entertainment. We performed two plays, one called "An April Fool," the other "Two in the Morning;" spliced the main brace, had some singing and dancing, and finished up with that good old farce "*Ici on Parle Français*," That's how the British Jack overcomes "the dangers of the sea and the violence of the enemy."

From there we went to Walfish Bay to meet our relief—the *Dwarf*, and bid farewell to the West Coast of Africa. We were about two years and a half in commission by this time, and not a bit sorry to go.

But before leaving "The Coast" altogether I must tell you about a little incident that I've often taken a quiet laugh over to myself. It occurred while coaling at one of these outlandish ports. They weren't all like Fernando Po, where the coal came aboard in lumps passed from hand to hand. At some places we lay a long way out and the stuff came in lighters, sometimes loose, sometimes in bags. It had all to be whipped aboard and the empty lighter sent back.

There were often long waits between the lighters, sometimes short ones. When a lighter arrived it was frequently the deuce's own job getting the coal out, on account of the ship rolling like an empty tub and threatening either to fall on top of you or suck you under at every heave. If the weather was wet—that put the finishing touch to it and the tale of misery was complete. Also, what should have been one ordinary day's cheerful work was turned into a long, dreary darg lasting about a week.

One afternoon the lighters were terribly erratic; the ship roll—roll—rolled horribly; a persistent drizzle kept us wet and cold and unspeakably miserable. With so much dust about we were all as grimy as Hood's coal-heavers "off the Wash." The worst of it was we took the muck below and made the lower deck as bad as the upper.

You would empty a lighter and "Pipe down" would go. Then you were no sooner down below in the mess than "Hands coal ship!" would sound again, and up you had to trudge.

Discomfort and irritation had the time of their lives. Everybody had the wind up and was ready to jump on everybody else.

As I was coming on deck in answer to one of these calls, grumbling to myself all the way, I saw, with the tail of my eye, that Billy, "The Bloke," was standing a little before the companion, evidently lying in wait for somebody to vent *his* ill-humour upon. Jack Durran, our diarist, was right behind me on the ladder, and grumbling much louder than I. Jack, however, didn't see Billy, nor had I time to give him warning, when he popped his head through the companion and said out loud, "It's about time this was paid off! "

Billy pounced on him at once. "What was that you said, Durran?"

Jack sprang to attention, and saluted. "Beg pa'd'n, si'"

"'What was that you said?' I say," snapped Billy, showing his teeth in a grin which added, "I've got you, anyway!"

Jack turned the face of a sheep to him and said, as genially as though he were telling him the time, "I was saying, sir"—here he put his tongue around his lips—"I was saying, sir, that the weather had been rotten lately."

Billy gave him one look, struck his telescope against his leg and stalked aft, leaving us to smother ourselves in coal dust quite happily that afternoon.

CHAPTER 22

Ups and Downs of Sea Life

We left the West Coast in a gale which blew us from Cape Town right away above the latitude of Campos, Rio de Janeiro—if you look at the map you'll see the distance—and here, after the storm died down, an incident took place which, in order to tell the story properly, and give you the full import of its pathos, and of its tragedy, I must go back to the second or third week of the commission.

It was one lovely morning just after sunrise, when we were jogging along under easy sail, on the way to Madeira. A fine, sweet breeze was pushing, and at the same time bringing over to us the scents of old and new Castile, where the grape and the orange and all the other delicious fruits of that sunny old clime would be in bloom, and they touched our lips with a flavour like champagne, and set our teeth watering for a taste of them in reality.

The middle watch—from 12 to 4 a.m.—had just been relieved, but the beauty of the morning kept all hands on deck. The sun rushed up over the eastern horizon like a revolving funnel, its outer rim quivering in a haze of brilliance, and its core so dazzling that the eye was blinded looking at it. The sky was a deep azure, flecked with long trailing feathers and tufts of gossamer cloud all delicately tinted in pink, green, mauve, salmon, orange, silky-white, and other lovely shades, which floated overhead like fairy sprites, had their photographs taken in the shining water below, and then changed colour and faded altogether while you looked at them. The ocean stretched away like a vast sheet of wavy glass with nothing ahead breaking its polished surface, while above the western rim hung piles and masses of thin, filmy mist, like thistledown, which broke up, as if blown upon from behind, and went floating out of sight like puffs of smoke from a pipe.

About an hour before the watch was called a sail had been sighted astern, and now a little brig began to come up with us hand over fist. From her trucks, which twinkled like brass buttons at her mastheads, to her bulwarks, she was dressed in snowy canvas. Every sail was full, and every additional stitch that could be useful—stun'sails, skysails, and what not—set, and helping to push, so that she came dancing over the blue water like a little girl skipping home from school. It was pretty to watch her bounding along, rising and falling with the gentle swell. She seemed to be new and was clipper-built. Her copper flashed like gold every time she lifted and the water at her stem frothed up like billows of wool, and then fell away from either bow in a ravishing little curl like the "kiss-me-quick" at a young lady's ear, and ran along her sides like festoons of glittering jewellery.

The sight of her took our breath away—she came so suddenly upon us, and looked so buoyant and free.

She seemed the very spirit of morning—light, airy, graceful, young and happy. She passed us with the swish of a racing yacht, not more than a cable's length distant. There wasn't a soul on her deck, but when she showed her stern we saw a man at the wheel, and behind him a lady in a blue blouse and with a light-coloured handkerchief round her neck, holding a baby in her arms. Seeing us all intently watching her, the lady (she would be the captain's wife, I daresay) held the baby towards us and dandled it up and down, whereat we gave them both a full-throated cheer. Then we caught the brig's name shining in gilt Roman letters just under the taffrail:

Lucy: London

and shouted after her, "Good luck to you, *Lucy*!" which the lady answered with another toss of the baby, and away they went as if borne on a summer cloud.

We watched the little fabric grow less and less till she was a mere speck, never thinking to see her again; then the watch went about their work, the others turned in, and we forgot the incident.

Well, that is the story; here is the sequel, two and a half years afterwards. I have told you how we had been driven over a thousand miles out of our course, but I couldn't describe the storm that drove us there.

The wind blew as if all the furies had been let loose. The seas ran in mad mountains, with the spume whirling around their tops like pine smoke. Sometimes we were perched on what appeared to be a boiling pit of black lava; at other times down we plunged into a deep trough with sickly green walls towering on either side threatening to topple over and crush the life out of us. The discomfort was frightful. The galley fire would not burn, and we could not get anything warm to eat or drink. Our bodies were sore all over from the broken water dashing against us. Everything was wet. Sleep was impossible in such a tumbling turmoil, even could we have turned in and lain among our sodden night- gear. But the *Swallow* was a staunch little craft and weathered it nobly without losing a spar. Fourteen days we had of this, the captain seldom leaving the poop during the whole time; and then one afternoon the wind dropped as suddenly as it had risen. All night the ocean moaned like a creature in pain. Next morning, with a leaden sky above and a sulky sea below, we set to work to dry up and get things put to rights.

The look-out man reported a sail on the starboard bow, which, as we drew nearer, we found to be a little brig. Her spars were anyhow. Her sails had been blown away, and what remained of them streamed like ragged ribbons from her yards. There was a look of dejection and utter melancholy about her, standing all alone in the gloom, that reminded you of a youngster who has lost herself.

As we came nearer, we saw that she was slowly foundering. Most of her upper works were gone, and the raffle hung about her sides trailing away like seaweed. We came nearer still, hailed her, and then fired a gun, but there was no answer, save the creak of her spanker-gaff, the vangs of which had been carried away, and the spar itself, swaying backward and forward, looked for all the world like the arm of a disabled sailor wildly beckoning for help, while his crazy, half-stifled voice lent its pitiful appeal.

She was abandoned.

She must have started a leak, which was too big for her people to cope with—we saw that by the fore and after pumps, which were both rigged—and they had left her. But when? There was no sign of them anywhere around, though the officers searched the whole horizon with their glasses. Certain sure they were all drowned. Perhaps we had floundered over the spot where they were now lying.

She was sinking before our eyes. We stood by and saw the water rise till her bulwarks were awash, every spar and timber about her crying like doomed children. Suddenly she gave a big sigh and a heave, and up came her stern. There, in faded gold letters, were the words:

Lucy: London

The sight of them sent a thrill through the ship. The uppermost thought in each of our minds was: "What about the woman and the baby? Were they saved, or what became of them?" I tell you we had a lot to conjecture and talk about that day. Of course, it was so long since we had first met the brig, and she might have taken twenty trips to different parts in that time, and changed hands as often. But you never know. That is sea life all the world over: here to-day and away to-morrow. You never know what will happen, and you've got to take things just as they come. No wonder that Jack is a careless, happy-go-lucky sort of soul. If he were to stop and think of the dangers that beset him he would never be able to live his life at all, and there would be few fur coats and feather hats in this little island of ours. So he merely laughs at them and hopes for the best.

We stood by, like men at a graveside, and watched her disappear, watched also the eddies caused by her sinking die out, leaving the sea unruffled as if nothing had happened, then turned, sad enough you may imagine, and steered for La Platte.

We thought as we went that, cruel as the sea is, there is yet a so-lemnity and dignity about her mode of burial that the most imposing ceremony in the richest cemetery ashore cannot equal. It is also the most appropriate and fitting end to a ship's or a sailor's life.

THE DOLDRUMS

Soon after our parting with the *Lucy*, the weather, satisfied, you would have thought, with the toll it had taken, seemed to make up its mind to be "good," and we had a fine spell of blue skies, sparkling breezes, and dancing water around us.

Then we ran into the Doldrums, and there we lay for another fortnight or so,

As idle as a painted ship
Upon a painted ocean.

spinning round and round on our keel, the masts boring a hole in the sky. If you threw a bottle over the starboard side at night you got it on the port-side in the morning. The sea was lovely to look at—rich deep blue, and as flat and clear as a looking-glass. If you bent over the side you saw the ship, with every detail to the pennant at the mast-head standing out clear like a photograph beneath you, and all sorts of strange-looking fish swimming in and out among the rigging. The sky, when you looked at it, which was not often, for the awnings were spread, and you preferred keeping under them, was like a huge metal basin turned upside down, of a purple colour, with a fiery ball blazing in the middle. We could hear the raucous cry of the albatross, and often saw that lordly bird planing, with never a shake of his wing, like a gigantic snowflake in the hazy ether above.

Sometimes the frigate-bird, or the bo'sun, would come proudly sweeping along, and you would see him take a sudden dive into the sea and come up with a big fish wriggling in his beak.

Another would chase him for it, and then you would see the two circling and whirling, feathers flying, the fish being dropped a dozen times and picked up as often before it reached the water—a regular battle-royal in fact. It was rare sport to watch the flying fish pursued by the dolphins, and the albatross hovering above to catch either of them when they came out of the water. Many a good breakfast we had of the flying fish which flopped aboard for shelter. Poor beggars! It was out of the water into the frying-pan for them, sure. We used to lure them aboard at night with the cook's lantern, and then there would be a feast around the fo'c'sle gun when the middle watch was called.

Sometimes whole fleets of "Portugee men-o'-war" would pop into view. These are tiny sea-creatures made of filmy blubber, which rise to the surface in very calm weather, and shine with a green light at night, like fireflies, only not so clearly—more like phosphorous. They are fitted with sails, which allow them to slip over the water, and can be raised or lowered at will. When the least hint of wind comes, they

Fold their tents, like the Arabs,
And as silently steal away.

It was interesting to watch them, though if you took one in your hand it seemed of no more substance than a soap-bubble. How they came to be named "Portugee men-o'-war" I have no idea, nor have I been able to find out.

Talk about sport and fun! We used to get a spare course over the side and make a pond of it—for the place was swarming with sharks— by belaying the clews inboard and tricing the head up with whips from the fore and main yards. Then the pipe would go "Hands to bathe!' and what a kick-up we would make! You would see the sharks— "sailor's homes" we used to call them—roaming around outside licking their lips. We caught four or five of these gentry. One of them was a monster, about eighteen feet long, and as thick round the middle as the main yard. We had some work before he was landed.

Then there was the turtle catching. Some of these brutes weighed nearly half a ton. Jack Da Costa, one of our *Kroomen*, was clever at turning them. When a turtle hove in sight, we found it sleeping as a rule. A boat would be quietly lowered and softly pulled over to the unsuspecting sleeper. Jack would then dive below him, and before you could wink there would be a floundering in the water, and over the brute would go, belly up, and his flappers whirling in the air. Then we whipped the stern painter round him, towed him back and hoisted him aboard, Jack meanwhile sitting on the gun'l beside the cox'n, with his teeth all showing in an ear-to-ear grin. After that we fed like aldermen for the next few days. But the heat was cruel, and we couldn't sleep at night for want of air, so that we were all glad when at last we got edged out of the belt of calms and off again on our course.

CHAPTER 23

Our Entertainers

One of the pleasantest features of the cruise that I love to recall now, when sitting by the fireside of an evening, is the entertainments that came off during our long trips at sea—very often in harbour, too, especially at Monte Video, where we had big audiences of ladies and gentlemen to hold forth before. The captain, as I have said, was a good reader; his name often figured on our programmes.

Billy, the first lieutenant, could sing, but was too affected: wouldn't let himself go. One night he gave us "Nancy Lee," and the rousing chorus that followed each verse ought to have drawn him out, and warmed him up besides; but it didn't. Next day one of the fellows piped:

See, there she stands upon her hands
And waves the key!

which Billy, unluckily, heard, and would sing no more. He thought they were making game of him forward.

Mr. Baynham, the Navigating Master, had a humorous turn. Two of his songs I remember well—perhaps because of both the tunes being Scotch. He used to rig up in a gown, by way of surplice, and deliver them as the parson does in church. This way, with a nasal intonation:

"Brethren; we will now sing the one thousand one hundredth and onety onth ps-a-a-lm—beginning at the beginning:

Tune: "Scotch."
("Ye Banks and Braes o' Bonnie Doon.")

There were three crows sat on a tree,
And they were black as black could be!
(Sing!)
Those crows, desirous to be fed,

The one unto the other said—
(Sing!)
"There is a horse on yonder plain
Who some time lately hath been slain.
(Sing!)
We'll perch ourselves on his breast bone
And pick his eyes out one by one."
(Sing!)
Old hoss, old hoss, you've carried many passengers!
But now you'll be made into polony sassengers!

Amen!

The other was something after the same style:

Tune: "Auld Lang Syne."

There was a man; he had two sons
And these two sons were brothers:
Tobias was the name of one,
Sophias was the other's.

Now these two boys they had a coat;
They bought it on a Monday;
Tobias wore it all the week,
Sophias on the Sunday.

Now those two boys went to the field
The old grey colt to find;
Tobias he got up in front,
Sophias sat behind.

Now, those two boys went to the play
Whenever they thought fit:
Tobias in the gallery sat,
Sophias in the pit.

It came to pass that, one sad day,
These two poor brothers died,
They laid Tobias on his back
Sophias on his side!

Amen!

Mr. Richmond, the paymaster, was a comic too. He "came on" as the "dude," sucking the knob of his walking-stick. A great song of his, the tune a bright sparkling polka—I was playing it only yesterday—began:

One night in cold December,
I've reason to remember,
I fell in love with such a charming girl.
Her eyes were bright and tender,
Her waist was small and slender,
And her hair it hung around her head in curl.

Chorus:
And she said "Come, come,
Come along, old boy,
And don't you look so bashful and so shy,
For I am such a beauty,
And you must do your duty,
Or the magistrates will know the reason why."

It went on to relate how we took the young lady into an oyster shop where they consumed "seven score or more" between them, also some "pies and pawtaw." Then he turned sick and went to sleep. When he woke up he found his watch and chain and all his valuables gone. Moral: Have no truck with casual young ladies.

Another of the paymaster's songs was "Ten thousand miles away," a convict ditty. Lord! who hears these things nowadays, I wonder—though the stuff we get in present-day music halls is just as trashy, every bit, if not more so.

Mr. Richmond made a rare job of this song. Of course, it was the chorus that endeared it to us. Anything with a good chorus commends itself to a ship. This is how it went—the tune, another fine polka:

Sing ho, for a gay and a gallant barque,
A brisk and lively breeze,
A captain, too, and a bully crew
To carry me o'er the seas,
To carry me o'er the seas, my boys,
To my own true love, so gay,
She's taken a trip in a government ship,
Ten thousand miles away.

Chorus:
Then, blow ye winds, i-oh!
A roving I will go,
I'll stay no more on England's shore,
So let the music play.
I'll start by the morning train,

I'll cross the raging main,
For I'm on a voyage to my own true love,
Ten thousand miles away!

There were four or five more verses, but these are all I've room for. The chorus was one of our very best sea ditties, and we used to roar it out till we nearly had the yards down about our ears.

We had some good talent on the lower deck. Strange to say, Saturday is the day on which I am now writing this, and memory, taking a leap to the Saturdays in the *Swallow*, over a bridge of forty-six years, brings the scene back as clearly as though I had never left it. I see the bustle and activity, and hear the voices of my shipmates raised in hearty concert. Saturday was "scrub and wash lower-deck day." When all hands were below and the brushes going, somebody would start a song, say, "The Farmer's Boy," then the rest would take it up and the deck would ring.

When the crowd of us got started it was a scene to remember. Sixty men or so, most of them with nothing on but a pair of old trousers, and these tucked up till they resembled pants, working with scrubbing-brush, holystone, squeegee, drying-cloth and swab, their bodies glistening with sweat from their vigorous exertions and their voices roaring out some fine old melody—sea or shore, it was all the same to us provided the chorus was good—I tell you it was grand!

Today, I hear in fancy—sitting with the pen in my hand, the clock ticking an accompaniment—as clearly as I did then in reality, the joyful shout of triumph that rose with the last verse:

In course of time he grew a man,
And the good old farmer died.
He left to the lad the farm that he had,
And his daughter for his bride.

So the boy who was, now a farmer is,
And he oftimes thinks with joy
Of the happy, happy day, when he came that way,
To be a farmer's boy.

Chorus: (like the burst of a brass band).
For to plough, and to sow, and to reap and to mow,
And to be a farmer's boy.
For to plough, and to sow, and to reap and to mow,
And to be a farmer's boy,
To be a farmer's boy!

Where are the owners of those hearty voices now, I wonder. Some sleeping peacefully in little village churchyards. Some, with the

Wild mob's million feet

trampling around them, but powerless to disturb their slumber, hid away in the large cemeteries of towns. Some, three to my certain knowledge, lashed up in their hammocks, with the round shot tied to their ankles, await the Last Trump in the natural sepulchre of the sailor. Some may be hearty still. Some, like the writer, scarce able to pipe a note, but making a good try. The old ship herself is broken up, her timbers scattered to the four winds of heaven. Nothing but memories remain.

Ah, well! These are sweet, anyway. And if man or thing leave sweet memories behind—*that* is all that matters!

We could all do our little bit at singing—in a way, of course—but Curly Millet led the choir. A sweet, tenor voice Curly had. He went in for fine stuff too: "Sally in our Alley," "Mary, call the cattle home," etc.

It was he, if you remember, who began the commission with "Isle of Beauty." But the song I liked best in Curly's collection was the "Three Fishers." First time I heard it he made me cry. Curly, however, was appointed Captain's steward in the room of the man who died, so we lost him in the fo'c'sle.

Fred Booth (Buntin) was another good singer, and a proper hero to me. An all-round handy man was Fred. He could make a signal, fire a gun, write a rhyme, paint a picture, sing a song, clap a sole on a boot, or make or patch a pair of trousers—anything that came his way. Fred was "Ready, ay Ready." And besides, he was a decent, genial, good-hearted buttie.

Three of the songs of his that I remember are "When the *Swallows* homeward fly," "Love, once again," and "Come into the garden, Maud," the latter rendered with great dramatic vigour and passion.

Westwater, his opposite number, had what I thought a wonderful *falsetto* pipe, which he could make flute-like at times. He was our "leading lady." His high tremolo notes used to ring all over the ship. I'll never forget his rendering of one of Haynes Bayly's songs: "We met, 'twas in a crowd." Standing with an agonised expression on his face, wringing his hands and shaking his lower lip, while his "Adam's apple" worked up and down like the safety-valve of our engine, he would spit out the words, something after this fashion:

We met-t-, t-t-was in a c-r-r-owd,
And I thought 'e-e-e would shun me!
I looked—I scarce could br-r-ee-e-ath
For his e-y-e-s we-re upon me!

I tr-ied!—oh, how I tr-i-e-d—
My feel-ee-ings to sm-other-r!
Oh! thou hast been the ca-a-use
Of this anguish—my mother-r-r!

Another of Bayly's songs that was a favourite aboard, also sung by Westwater, was "The Pilot."

Marchand, the ship's corporal, was our star turn. He had a large selection, both English and Irish, to choose from, the latter being his favourites. It was Marchie, bless him! who first introduced me to "Tim Finnigan's Wake," "Rory O'More," "The Rocky Road to Dublin," "Paddy Haggerty's leather breeches," "Widow Machree," and hosts of Moore's melodies that to forget now would bring more sorrow to me than the loss of my pension. He had also some fine, rollicking, descriptive ditties which he laid off in great style. . One was "Mr. Bob Tubbs," dealing with the troubles of a newly-married couple who got separated just when starting on the honeymoon. Another was "Sairey Ann," telling about a cook in Grosvenor Square who

… pined and pined away
For ten long years and a half, sir,
Sorrowing, sighing, day by day,
And never once did laugh, sir,
For one, Billy Kent, who, alas!
Is working under Government,
Engaged for fourteen years.

However, Bill gets out of prison on a ticket-of-leave, and

One fine day what does she see
Before the airy standing?
In ecstasy she cries "Tis he!'
And rushed up to the landing.

Bill is taken below to the kitchen, entertained royally, and then, to show his gratitude, walks off with the family silver and Sairey's poor little Geneva. But the policeman on the beat, who is a rival of Bill's, and on the watch, pounces on him, catches him redhanded, and Sairey, losing one lover, gains another, and all ends happily.

The corporal had a rich baritone voice, and a bland, graciously urbane manner—for singing! On duty—a different man altogether. *Then*, he was the policeman—"Navy "all the time! But get him up in the dog watch for a song and then he took you in his arms.

The most popular of his batch in the fo'c'sle was "Ratcliff Highway," to the tune called "The Ash Grove." I think I see him standing on the fore-hatch, arms outspread as if embracing everybody, face lifted to the sky, body bent forward, eyes half shut, and a positive sob in his voice:

I love her dear mother,
I'm fond of her brother,
On sister and father I spend half my pay,
But oh! give me Nancy,
The girl of my fancy,
To go for a ramble down Ratcliff Highway!

The chorus was the last three lines repeated, and didn't we roll them out!

But the one *I* liked best of all, which usually came as an encore to "Ratcliff Highway," was "Peggy of Sweet Coleraine." You should have heard him singing this song, and all of us chiming in, with Westwater in the high alto. When Marchand was "up," the officers were irresistibly drawn forward as if by magnet, so that everybody in the ship shared, and was happy. I don't know the name of the tune, but it is a very popular melody—Welsh, I think. I've heard it sung to two different sets of verses—"Donnachy's Wake," and "The charming young widow," but neither of these is as good as Marchand's. This was our pet verse:

Oh, well I remember the night that we parted,
The moon shone serenely and calm was the air;
I told her my love, and we both were light-hearted,
And Peggy she promised my fortune to share.
'Neath the old cabin thatch, which shelters the starling,
I kissed her and kissed her again and again—
Oh, sad is my heart when I think of my darling,
My tender young Peggy of sweet Coleraine!

Bill Grimshaw was our pet elocutionist. Bill was leading stoker; a tall man, standing over six feet high and as thin as one of his own cinder-rakes. He had a large *repertoire*—mostly sea-pieces: "Jack Oakum," "Sunday at Sea," "Two Hearty Tars," "Jack and the Jew," etc. "The Sailor's Apology" was also on his list, but that piece, being the

153

captain's, was taboo before the mainmast. We rigidly adhered to that principle: whoever sang a song, or did anything else, first, that item belonged to him right through the commission.

But Bill had plenty without it. He had had an accident to his left eye at one time—through a boiler explosion—which wrinkled that side of his face, giving it a sort of surprised expression. This added the finishing touch to the drollery of his reciting. Among all his pieces "Jack Oakum" was my favourite.

I've never come across it since I left the Service, either in print or by hearing it recited. But I know all the words, and as there is a nice salt flavour about them, recalling the old "Wooden Wall" days, and, as the piece isn't long, I'll just set it down and you can enjoy the yarn for yourself.

But, alas! I can't reproduce Grimshaw's manner of delivery. That is a great drawback. However, here it is:

Jack Oakum was a seaman good,
As ever stood to gun,
And, when on shore, was always first
To have a bit of fun.

One night near Plymouth Dock he strolled;
A play-bill met his eye,
On which THE TEMPEST was announced,
In letters six feet high.

Now, Jack had never seen a play,
But to join the folk was willin',
So straightway he went up aloft,
For which he paid one shillin'.

The curtain rose, the play commenced,
In thunder, lightning, rain;
A gallant ship, with many souls,
Was instant rent in twain.

That moment all the gallery props
Gave way in sudden fit,
And avalanched that motley crew
Right headlong in the pit!

"Well, well," says Jack; "If this be play
I will this instant strike it.
It may be play for aught I know,
But, damn me if I like it!"

Jack went to sea, and fought the French,
Came back with pockets lined,
And jumped ashore, rejoiced to meet
The old friends left behind.

He took a trip to London town,
Where everything is gay,
And strolled to Dairy's lofty walls—
THE TEMPEST was the play!

"Ha! here's the stuff for me," says Jack,
Determined to be jolly,
But this time he went to the pit,
Remembering former folly.

And when the well-known scene arrived,
And lightning rent the skies,
Jack slued around, and turned his quid,
And upward cast his eyes—

"Hold hard aloft, you jolly dogs!
You howling, jovial parties!
Mind what you're at, you shillin' swabs,
For—down you come, my hearties!"

Umbray, the ship's cook, had a song called "The Hills of Chile," a fine "up-anchor" ditty this was: made the capstan spin. It detailed the love affair of a Spanish young lady, who was being courted by an American Naval Officer, to whom her mother strongly objected. I've tried everywhere to find this song—hunted library after library, bored into all sorts of collections, compilations and compendiums of old sea chanties, but have never caught a glimpse of it. I'm sorry for this, for it is a fine specimen of the fo'c'sle ditty of my day. I remember only this one verse of it:

Oh, mother, dearest mother,
How can you run them down?
For these American men are gentlemen,
And men of high renown.
Those American men are gentlemen,

And their hearts are bold and free,
And I'll cross the Hills of Chile with them,
And fight for libertie.
With me fal-th-dal lal-th-dal ay,

155

With me fal-th-dal lal-th-dal a-a-a-a-ay.

The last "ay" had five beats all to itself. Umbray used to stand outside the swifter pulling and singing for all he was worth, while we in the race bent to the bars and made the capstan whirl. Perhaps some of the old "Swallows" may see this—perhaps Umbray himself may be alive—if so, it will recall old times and set them humming.

Another fine old song was "Away down Rio" (pronounced "Ry-o"). I've met this one often enough, but never the way we sang it. It wasn't used by us merely as a chorus, but was tacked on to a pure Navy ditty, called "Around Cape Horn." This way:

Our ship had been inspected
By the Adm'ral all around,
While lyin' in Portsmouth Harbour—
That large and beautiful town.

We were waitin' there for orders,
For to sail away from home,
Our orders were for R-i-o,
And then around Cape Horn.

Chorus:
Then away down Rio,
Away down Rio,
Then, fare you well, my bonnie young girl,
We're bound for Rio Grande.

When we arrived at Rio
We tarried there a while;
We set up all our riggin',
And bent all our new sail:
From ship to ship they cheered us,
As we did sail along,
And wished us pleasant weather
A-rounding of Cape Horn.

Chorus: *Then away, etc.*

At last we rounded the Horn, my boys,
Five nights and five days,
And the next place we dropped anchor
Was Valiparaiso Bay,
Where the pretty little girls they do come down,
With their dark and curly hair—

They are the loveliest of girls,
I vow and do declare!

Chorus: *Then away, etc.*

They love a jolly sailor,
When he is on the spree,
He calls for liquor merrily,
And spends his money free.

And when that money is all gone,
They will not you impose—
They are unlike some girls we know,
Who go and sell your clo'es!

Chorus: *Then away, etc.*

Then, here's to Valiparaiso,
And all the natives there.
Likewise to all those pretty little girls
With their long and curly hair.
And if ever I live to get paid off,
I will sing from night till morn—
"God bless those pretty little Spanish girls,
That we met around Cape Horn!"

Chorus:
Then, away down Rio,
Away down Rio,
Then fare you well, my bonnie young girl,
We're bound for Rio Grande.

Lord! what choruses some of these old sea songs have. They mount and soar in swelling billows of melody, rolling waves of glorious sound that fill the ship fore and aft, flooding it in harmony; reverberating among the cordage, echoing and re-echoing from the sails aloft till the soul of a man is absolutely filled with rapture. Their words carry you to the ends of the earth, and back from there to the scenes of your boyhood, and home and friends, who are waiting with yearning hearts to grip you by the hand, just as you yourself are yearning to grip theirs.

And now these dear old anthems are never heard at all they tell me. Commissions are so short. Nobody pulls on anything; you just touch a button and steam does all the work.

Well, I'm sorry to hear it, for if that is the case, sea life, to my thinking, has lost about the only real delight that made it worth following.

This one: "We'll soon sight the Isle of Wight, my Boys," one of the very best of our homeward-bounders, I have heard a whole fleet sing at the same time. One ship started it, another took it up, and away it went right round the lot, covering miles of sea-water, the sound rising, billow upon billow, wave upon wave, like some mighty organ pealing to heaven.

This happened out in the roads off Monte Video, one night when our present King, George V. and his brother, Clarence, were on their tour round the world, and the *Bacchante* and her crowd met us there. There would be at least twenty ships round about—some American men-o'-war, too, if I'm not mistaken—the *Shenandoah* and the *Massachusetts*—and they also joined in. If the prince happened to be aboard, I'm sure the King will remember it. That night the very stars seemed to sing!

I can't recall the whole song, but here is the last verse and the chorus:

(You are to suppose yourself in, say, the *Swallow*, while the man who has started the song is in the *Garnet*, or one of the other ships. You wait till the first four lines are sung, and then join in when the chorus comes round.)

And now we're paid off,
And happy are we,
With a glass in each hand,
And a lass on each knee!

Chorus:
We'll soon sight the Isle o' Wight, my boys,
We'll soon sight the Isle o' Wight, my boys,
If the breezes don't fail!
If the breezes don't fail!

In the *Swallow*, this song belonged to Harry Watson, our next best singer to Curley Millet, and a born musician. He couldn't read a note of music, but knew how a song ought to be sung all right. Harry was a bit of a wag. It was he who used to say he liked having the toothache because he felt so well after it left. Harry had a fine voice and some good songs, the best I liked being "The Four Jolly Smiths," which he sang with great vim.

He usually acted as conductor in the choruses, wielding a belaying-pin for a baton, while going through the motions and keeping us in time like a regular Landon Ronald. The great difference between Harry and that prince of conductors being that, when things went wrong, he never tore his *own* hair—it was always the hair of the party who caused the trouble. As the belaying-pin was made of *lignum-vitae*, and weighed a couple of pounds or so, you hadn't to be near him if you made a bad note or, by gum, you remembered it.

I see him now: a little, stout, merry-faced fellow from Lancashire—a "Red Roser," as he used to say—who sang like a nightingale. The last verse (which I quote from memory) was his especial favourite—as it was with all of us. As he sang it, you would have thought he was cuddling the words, if you take my meaning, while at the end of the chorus, the way he kept us hanging on to the high note of the "rolling," before he gave the signal to drop and finish, was fine:

The four jolly smiths, when their hair turns grey,
Will gladly sit down and rest,
And merrily each one of them will say:
"We've done our very, very best!"

And the thought so dear will each bosom cheer—
Let the young smiths still strike on,
And feed well the fires of their resting sires,
As the four jolly smiths have done!

Chorus:
With the bang, and the clang,
And the ring, ding, dong,
The work goes merrily rolling along.
With the bang, and the clang,
And the ring, ding, dong,
The work goes merrily rolling—along!

Harry sometimes got the nickname of "Old Polish," which came to him through a passage he had with the first lieutenant. One day, at gun inspection, Billy spotted a dull compressor on the 7-inch gun.

"Whose part of the gun is this?" said "The Bloke," tapping the steel plate with his telescope.

Watson, who was standing at his elbow, saluted.

"Is this your compressor?"

"Yes, sir."

"Look at it."

Harry looked—"Beg y' pardon, sir; what's the matter with it?"

"Why, it isn't clean. Can't you see it?"

"Not clean, sir! Why, I cleaned it not five minutes ago.

Billy jerked in his monocle, "Don't repeat my words, sir!" he barked. "I say it isn't clean. . . . Dull as a doormat!"

"Oh, dull, sir, may be, beg y' pardon. . . . But quite clean . . . not polished."

"Well, polish it, then! . . . I'll polish you! . . . Report!" And round the gun went Billy, finding fault with everybody.

Harry got five days 10A. for that little play of fancy.

I had a turn myself once for much the same thing. I mustered at Divisions one day in a pair of trousers which had a stain on them. Billy noticed this and gave me a rounding. Never thinking to be "smart," I said that these weren't the trousers I had down below in my locker.

"Oh," said Billy, "Aren't they? Very good! V-e-r-y good, indeed!— Corporal! Five nights first watch for Noble, which will give him time to make up some more of his excellent jokes!"

"First watch" punishment consisted of standing under the bell for one hour in the last dog, where you were supposed to think. A good deal of that was done, too, principally about Billy.

Of course, I had my own little chirp occasionally. I was rather timorous to start, because my voice was poor, and the only songs I knew were Scotch. But I found mine were just as well received as any. Three, in particular, won high favour: "The Boatie Rows," "The poor but honest Sodger," and "Willie brewed a peck o' maut"—sung to Masterton's tune. This was a prime favourite. To hear the lower deck ringing with the chorus would have warmed your heart:

We are nae fou', sae very, very fou',
But juist a wee drappie in our e'e,
The cock may craw, the day may daw',
But aye we'll taste the barley bree!

CHAPTER 24

In the Dog-watches

Another glorious, heart-filling song of Harry Watson's was "Drink to me only with thine eyes." He taught us a humming accompaniment to this one. When Curly Millet was off duty, he usually took the melody, Harry and others following, with Westwater in the alto soaring above everybody. When all the parts were going, and the song rolling in lovely cadences, the ear was simply ravished with it. That chap Westwater used to send his high notes whirling about among the royal trucks in a way that was splendid to hear. If you happened to be aloft doing a job, you couldn't get on with your work for listening and waiting for them.

And we had some grand concerts. Nothing high-class, but just the simple, hearty kind that filled the hearts of us common sailor-men with great happiness, making life very pleasant for us. And, besides, they have left an impression on me that will never be rubbed out till the cold hand of death wipes the slate clean of everything.

Speaking about these concerts brings back memories of all the old songs we used to sing—songs you never hear nowadays, but which were very popular in my time, and must have been in vogue hundreds of years before then.

For instance, there was "The dark-eyed sailor," with its rolling chorus:

For the dark-eyed sailor,
For the dark-eyed sailor,
That sailed away from home.

Then "The Lowlands Low" was another fine one. The note of sadness—tragedy rather—running through it gave it a special appeal:

Oh, the boy beat his breast,

And away he did swim,
He swam till he came to
That gallant ship again,
Crying "Master, master pick me up,
Or else I shall be drowned,
For I'm sinking in the Low—lands—Low—lands,
For I'm sinking in the Lowlands low!"

You seem to hear voices long silenced in the grave rolling out the pathetic words.

Take "My love William." This was a special favourite with us, though, strange to say, without a chorus. It seems to be a version of Gay's "All in the Downs," or "Black-eyed Susan"—or was Gay's ballad a version of it?—Nobody can tell. These old sea songs seem to have been handed down from the time men first went to sea: passed from lip to lip for generations long before printing was thought of. Every time you meet them they're differently dressed. Look at "Away down Rio." I've come across this song twenty times, each time different. But the theme and the tune as a rule are the same.

So too with "My love William." Any old sailor you'll find with the song on his lips, but the words different.

Here is the way we sang it:
Oh, father, father, build me a boat,
That on the ocean I may float,
Hail every vessel that I pass by,
Saying "Have you heard of my sailor boy?"

She hadn't been long upon the deep,
When a man-o'-war she chanced to meet—
"Stop, stop that ship, you joyful crew,
For I fear my William's on board of you!"

"What colour of clothes did your William wear?
What colour of hair was your William's hair?"
"A light blue jacket and trousers white,
And the colour of his hair was my heart's delight."

"Oh, no, fair lady he is not here,
I fear he lies drowned at yonder pier,
At yonder pier as I passed by
It was there I left your poor sailor boy."

She wrung her hands and she tore her hair,
Just like a lady in despair,

162

And she threw herself upon the deep,
Crying, "My love William, are you asleep?"

Another fine old rouser that nobody knows the age of is "Windy Weather." This must have cheered our remote ancestors, just as it did poor Tom Hood—the only song he was ever known to sing. It contains at least forty verses, all dealing with life on board ship, and every fish in the sea is made to do duty. This is how it goes—many a time I've waltzed to it, feeling the lift of the wave in its glorious melody:

The girls are a-weeping, the anchor's away;
Then up came the dog-fish that swims in the bay,
Crying, "Windy weather! Stormy weather!
While the wind blows we'll haul together!"

Then up came the eel, with his slippery tail,
Crying, "I'll go aloft, boys, and loose all your sail,
For it's" etc.

Then up came the lobster, with his thorny back,
Crying, "I'll take the fo'c'sle and board the fore-tack,
For it's" etc.

Then up came the cod-fish, with his chuckle head,
Crying, "I'll take the chains, boys, and heave you the lead.
For it's" etc.

Then up came the flat-fish, that lies on the ground,
Crying, "Damn your eyes, Chuckle-head, mind how you sound!
For it's" etc.

Then up came the porpoise, with his bottle snout,
Crying, "Muster all hands, and we'll put her about!
For it's" etc.

Then up came the herring, the King o' the sea,
Crying, "Let fly your head sheets, it's ' Helum's-a-lee!'
For it's" etc.

And so on, and on, and on! I've known us to go on warbling this ditty throughout the best part of a dog watch, and then not be tired of it.

That's how we drove dull care away till Monte Video hove in sight and we dropped anchor in the harbour, glad to have a steady deck under our feet again, and a chance of a leg-stretcher ashore, having been tumbled about on salt water for forty-four days. There was always plenty of work, plenty of drill—Lord knows there was any amount of that, night and day—and a sing-song in the evening if the weather was fine. If not, then out with your sewing or "guivory" (fancy) work: never an idle moment.

Sometimes a man read a book aloud, or a story from one of the magazines, another man taking his sewing, knitting or whatever he was at, while he read. This reading aloud was usually my job. In this way we got through a lot of novels of one kind and another; Miss Braddon, I remember, being our favourite author.

One night, wet on deck, we were all in the mess, quietly reading or going on with the job in hand. Sharkie Bradford, who was a great reader of penny novelettes, was sitting beside me, with a candle in front of him, devouring one of his pet yarns. Nobody was speaking. All of a sudden Sharkie jumped up, banged the table with his fist, shouted "I knew it!—I knew it!" and instantly became absorbed in the story again, leaving us all nearly startled out of our wits. He had been working out the plot in his own mind, and it had shaped just as he thought it would.

Another night I was reading one of Dickens's stories aloud, where a horrible murder is committed, and the feelings of the murderer delineated with great force and power. It was *Martin Chuzzlewit*. We were all deep in the story when Sharkie interrupted, saying in a hollow voice, "The bloke wot wrote that there yarn was a murderer himself, boys, to my way of thinking."

"How do you make that out?" he was asked.

"Why, look how he can tell about it. How could he picture the thing so well if he hadn't done a bloody murder himself?"

This set us all thinking for a minute. Presently I lifted my eyes from the book and said, "If that's the case, Sharkie, you must be a murderer, too."

"Me! How?"

"Because, how can you know he's describing a murder properly unless you've done one yourself?"

"Aha!" cried the other fellows, "that's one for you, Sharkie!—Go on, Jock."

Another favourite was Wilkie Collins, but some of his yarns were so gruesome that we were afraid to go on deck after hearing them read. What we liked best were love yarns—not too spooney—something with a sailor-man as the hero; the heroine a nice little girl in a cottage on a cliff, waiting for him to come home and be married. But she had to be True Blue. If she were shifty or flighty or feather-headed—take her away! While if there were too much "slush" in the story somebody flung a wet swab at the reader and knocked his candle out.

Some of the men were good yarn-spinners themselves. Our sail-maker, "Sails" we called him, I don't remember his real name, was the best we had. Some of his yarns, however, were so highly spiced that we would hardly allow them to pass muster, although Sails swore them to be gospel truth. He usually introduced them by saying, "When I was in the last ship," which was a right Nelson touch of his, as, we being all shipmates for the first time, he knew that nobody could trip him up. Sails was getting on in the Service. He wore spectacles to read or sew with, although, as he used to say, he could see a fly at the mast-head.

When a Doubting Thomas brought him up in a yarn he would look at him over the rim of his glasses and say, "Didn't I mention that this 'ere took place when I was in the last ship?"

"Course you did."

"Will you there?"

"No, an' biddy well you know it."

"Well, what the 'ell are you pokin' yer nose in for? . . . All you've got to do is listen. D'ye think a man's a liar?"

"Oh, no," Thomas would answer. "I don't *think*. I *know*"

But he met his match one day in the town (Monte Video), and I was glad to be present and see him bowled over. (I shouldn't wonder if you've heard this story before, for it was written out and sent home to one of the newspapers.)

There was a snug little *café* in the Calle de 25 de Mayo where the "Swallows" used to meet often. It was run by an Italian called Rodrigo, a pleasant, obliging fellow. We got a nice dinner there, finishing up with an omelette and a bottle of wine for half a dollar.

The bar took a semi-circle round two sides of the room, leaving a wide floor space. The windows, shaded with thin red curtains, looked into the street, so that you had a view of the people passing, and that was what we liked. There was also a nice little dancing-hall, with a good string band, and some pretty girls, too. That was another point in its favour.

One afternoon, there would be about a dozen of us in having a snack. The only other occupant besides ourselves was an American sailor, who lay tilted back on a chair with his feet on the counter, smoking.

While we were eating, a man came rushing in and told the land-lord that a great swarm of locusts had fallen upon the fields just outside the town, and had gone off, leaving not a green blade behind them. This led to a discussion, during which Hughie M'Ghee, one of the Marines, remarked that he often wondered why Providence created such pests, whose only mission in life seemed to be to harass and annoy people.

"Annoy people!" exclaimed Sails, turning upon him. "A lot you know about it! Why man, when I was in the last ship a crowd of these 'ere warmints comes off from the land, and afore you could wink, blowed if they ain't got every stitch of canvas clean out of her!"

At this the American turned slowly round, took the pipe from his mouth, pointed it at Sails, and said in a lazy drawl: "Brothers, I endorse that statement of yours. For, being on the high seas at the time, I met that same crowd of locusts, and every one of 'em had on a pair of canvas pants!"

Monte Video was a fine port to lie at in those days, far and away the best we found in all our rambles. Here we lived like fighting-cocks! Eggs were 3d. a dozen—or was it 2d.?—mutton 1½d. a lb., beef a 1d.; other provisions in proportion. Admiralty rations being much dearer, we left them behind, and took up the money instead. We were thus enabled to stock the messes with substantials, and go in for dainties besides—butter, cheese, a bottle of vinegar or sauce, jams and all sorts of sweet-tooth things. You could even get your rasher of bacon for breakfast at little extra cost.

There was a general grocery store close by the pier where all the provisions were got. This was kept by a little man called "Dirty Dick," a swarthy, dark-skinned Maltee, who was forever smiling.

First when we came to the place we used to go to Dirty's for a dinner or a snack. But one day Ginger White got a bit of the last man's egg on his plate—not much, but just enough to sicken him—and showed it to the other fellows. Sailors, as a rule, are not particular as to what goes into their stomachs, but even the minutest remains of some other person's breakfast on the plate you are eating your dinner off would, I should think, "scunner" anybody. So that finished us with Dirty. We went to Rodrigo's afterwards, where everything was served spotless.

I liked Monte Video. There were fine walks round the town, and strange flowers grew at the sides of the roads. A band used to play in the Grand Plaza every evening; and I liked to roam about inside the cathedral—whose domes towered high above the flat roofs of the town—where there were fine pictures, statuary, stained glass, altars, and so forth. One never tired of looking at them, and noting the different forms of worship taking place at the various shrines.

I fell in with a girl here who very nearly had me. A dark-eyed beauty she was—dark, flashing eyes that pierced you like a knife one minute and warmed you like a sunbeam the next—with a wealth of jet black hair that fell about her like an inky wave. Amelina was her name. Her father was organist of the cathedral, a Scot, hailing from Paisley; her mother, a Castilian—or had been, for she was dead.

Amelina was their only child. She took a great fancy to me, as did her father, who wanted to buy me off. But I was "ow'r young to marry yet," and besides, had a girl of my own, not to mention a preference for "a cat o' my ain kind." Her father, who was a burly, dignified-looking gentleman, with soft, dreamy grey eyes, and a massive head covered with grey hair, seemed to be pretty well off, as he lived in his own house on the outskirts of the town, where I got a hearty welcome every time I called. Sometimes he would take Amelina and me down to the cathedral and play the organ to us. Sometimes she and I went by ourselves. I liked to hear him, and used to wheedle him, both at home and in the cathedral, into playing the old Scotch songs and psalms.

To this day I never hear "Oh, wert thou in the cauld blast," but the cathedral of Monte Video, with Amelina and me standing by the organ, her father, who is playing, wagging his bushy head from side to side in ecstasy; the forms kneeling around the altars, and that lovely piece of music swelling through the arches comes dancing into my mind. With that memory comes another—how deliciously it sounded there. You never realize how sweet the songs of your own country can be till you hear them far away from home. There they speak to you with a different meaning altogether.

CHAPTER 25

The Bo'sun's Love Story

The South East Coast of America station was miles ahead of Africa in interest as well as comfort. Hardly a week passed without some striking incident happening to enliven it. For instance: a Revolution was "on" at Buenos Ayres while we were there, and we took part in quelling it. We had a paper chase at Colonia del Sacramento, were taken through Liebig's great meat factory at Fray Bentos (where I secured a couple of lovely buffalo horns); and had the good fortune to see a magnificent Lunar Bow one very dark midnight on the River Parana, and a fine Mirage coming down the Uruguay. Dropping South, we met the Patagonians, the Tierra del Fuegians and the penguins, saw the Southern Cross, and the Magellan Clouds in all their wonder and beauty, touched at Port Stanley in the Falkland Islands, where we met "oor ain folk" and gave them a theatrical concert. This cruise we repeated half a dozen times, and never without adventure—indeed, the latter half of the commission was full of it.

But by far the sweetest incident of all my *Swallow* days is the one I am going to tell you now. It happened on the last trip from the Falklands to Buenos Ayres. It might have been yesterday, I remember it so well. Indeed, it took such a grip of me that I have only to shut my eyes and lie back in my chair to live it all over again.

A STARRY NIGHT OFF PATAGONIA

It was a beautiful night in the middle watch. I had the first wheel, from 12 to 2. The sky was alight with stars. From zenith to horizon

All the heavens seemed to twinkle
With a crystalline delight.

making it clear above, but inky black below, there being no moon. The weather was very cold, for we were in the latitude where Craddock, poor chap, lost the number of his mess (and where, too, he was so worthily avenged, thank heaven!)

We were under all plain sail, and steering "full and by" on the starboard tack. The wind was true, that is, blowing with a constant force, and we were skimming over the unseen water, about eight knots to the hour, as steady as a church, with just a little heel to port. The *Swallow* was a fine sailer, and easily steered by a single helmsman; it was only when she had a heavy wind abaft the beam driving her that she needed two.

This was one of the nights that make you glad to be alive—fresh, crisp and full of ozone. You felt the blood tingling within you, and were fit to eat the spokes of the wheel. In fact that was my only objection to those nights; they made me so fearfully hungry, and there was so little to meet the demand!

When I took over the wheel, my instructions were to keep the t'gallant sail full, and to steer by a star that glimmered outside the weather leech. If I came up too near and blotted the star out altogether the sail lifted, and that was my warning to keep off.

My favourite trick was the wheel, and steering under such conditions what I liked best of all. To me it was like playing bo-peep with somebody in another world. I used to wonder if there really were live people up there as they say there are, and if they can see our habitation as we see theirs. All sorts of strange and high fancies would come into my head at such times, and I would feel as if I were at church with the organ pealing and all the people singing.

It's a glorious place to be on, the sea, on a clear dark night such as you get down around those parts. The loneliness is immense. You never feel such an atom, such a poor, insignificant, helpless morsel of creation anywhere as you do down with nothing but the stars around you, and such hosts of them.

And the mystery of it! The feeling that myriads and myriads of other atoms, under you and above you, all as wonderfully formed and perfectly adapted to their places as you are yourself, are living their lives, working out their destiny and serving their purpose equally as well as you, and in the same darkness being guided and protected by Something, and all as important seemingly, and of as much value in the sight of that Something as you are, big though you think yourself.

Sometimes I felt that my head would crack with the thoughts that came into it.

And then the majesty of such a night at sea! The overpowering—

solemnity of it, the sublime grandeur! It fills a man's mind with awe, and compels him to think high. He *must* forget the petty matters he is in the habit of thinking about during the day. At such a time he floats in regions far above earthly influence and is, I am convinced, nearer to God than ever he will be till he goes to Him altogether. Indeed, there's nothing I know of will more readily lift the soul of a man in adoration to his Maker than standing on a lonely deck on such a night, with only the cordage of a ship between him and heaven. The smoke of a steamer spoils the charm completely. A sailing-ship's the thing if you want to think properly.

Another quality I have always liked about the sea is this: it makes a man young and keeps him so. It is often remarked that sailors are simple and, as a rule, God-fearing. That, I'm sure, is the effect of such nights as the one I am speaking about. You cannot see *outwardly*, but you can *inwardly*, and you are made to think. This night was so dark that I couldn't see the deck I was standing on.

STEERING BY A STAR

I was enjoying my "trick," feeling elevated, glorified. Much as the shepherds in that Wonderful Old Story must have felt while they were being led to Everlasting Peace. Watching the star edging into and drawing away from the leech of the sail, I was humming to myself a little song my mother was fond of singing:

The stars are bright this beautiful night,
But when the moon appears,
They'll fade as soon as lamps at noon
The glory that she bears!

The stars are dull, the moon at full
Has now her course begun.
Her light will fail, her orb grow pale
Before the glorious sun!

when a voice at my side said, "Who's at the wheel?"

"Noble, sir."

"Oh, it's you, Jock!"

It was the bo'sun. He was very friendly with me, and I liked him immensely. He knew it, too, though I had never told him.

"How's she steering; steady, eh?"

"Oh, steady as a clock, sir."

"Lovely night, ain't it? Fine breeze, too; we're bowling along; did eight-and-a-half last log."

I watched my bonnie wee guide ahead, and winked at her. She kept bobbing in and out of the sail like a bright little guardian angel cautioning me to be careful. For all his friendliness, he might jump down my throat if I let the ship come up or fall off even half a point, and I wasn't going to give him the chance.

He walked to the bulwarks and came back.

"Makes you think of home, Jock, a night like this, don't it?"

"It do, sir; that's just where my thoughts were when you came for'ard."

He took another turn.

"Are you married, Jock?"

"Oh, sir!" I cried, feeling myself blush in the dark, and so flustered that I brought the ship up in the wind and nearly put the t'gallant sail aback. "Oh, sir! give us a chance!"

Fancy having a question like that fired at you, and you only a little over nineteen years old—and hadn't even seen a white girl for at least two of them. I was all abroad!

"Steady, oh!" said Tommy, reaching his hand over and pushing the wheel up a couple of spokes, "steady, my lad."

He stepped back for a minute and looked ahead till my little friend twinkled into view again. Then back he came.

"It's all right, Jock," he said, and his voice trembled; "It's all right. I beg your pardon. It was silly of me. But I forgot for the moment. You're too young; of course, of course. Ah-h! . . ."

This was a big sigh.

He stumped to and fro from the wheel to the ship's side, sending his glance ahead and astern and all over the ship, as I felt rather than saw, then stopped beside me once more.

"Jock," he resumed, "what made me ask you that question, d'ye think?"

"I couldn't say, sir," I answered; thinking to myself, "he's a bit confidential tonight," and winking to the star with my off eye.

"Well, it was because I got married myself just before I left England."

"Is that so, sir?" I said, with sudden interest, but keeping my eye on that weather leech; the star bobbing around at every swing of the mast as if saying "Keek! I'm listening!"

"Yes; just a couple of weeks. . . . My boy, it's a great thing to be married!"

"It must be, sir," I assented, smiling up at the star, who nodded

"Keek! Keek!" and seemed to smile back in return.

"It is. But, Lord! . . . Fancy being torn away just at the very start. . . . It's sickening, I call it . . . devilish! Such a nice little girl, too; sweet, charming, pretty, and oh! high above me . . . miles! . . . a proper little lady she is . . . tch! tch!"

His voice quivered with emotion, and came out with a growl like a wounded mastiff. I could see his shape, but not his face, it was so dark: but I had an idea what it would be like—tenderness, longing, woebegoneness, and all sorts of trouble working in it at the same time. Had one of My Lords of the Admiralty, whom he looked upon as the cause of his misery, chanced to get his nose between the bo'sun's second and third finger at that moment . . . pity him!

He leaned over with the heave and impatiently spat in the scuppers, then went on.

"That sweet little thing you're steering by reminds me of her—just the right sort of light for guiding a man she is . . . Ah-h-h!"

Another sigh, bigger than the last.

"Keek! Keek!" said the star. "Poor Tommy!"

"See how she dances round the leech of that sail," he continued. "That's exactly how my little wife does with me: always skipping around with her little caressing ways, and singing, and filling the house with her laughter. . . .

"Oh, Jock!" he burst out, shuffling with his feet, "you don't know anything about it! I hope this biddy commission will soon be over and let me get back to her. I feel her little hands tugging at my heartstrings—'struth I do: you've no idea what a pull it is, Jock! . . ."

I murmured something in sympathy, and the star twinkled and danced ahead as if in an ecstasy—"Keeki Keek!" it seemed to say—"Come on; follow me—I'll bring you there!"

The bo'sun strode over to the scuppers, expectorated again—I plainly heard his disgust expressed in the operation and came back: "She made me these. . . ."

WHAT LOVE CAN DO

"These" were a pair of beautiful knitted gloves, which he thrust into the light of the binnacle so that I could see them. They looked to me to be two pairs in one; the inside being soft white fleecy wool, the outside dark grey, and felt thick, warm and cosy. The work was finely executed, and the materials of the very best; and the suggestion that they had been a labour of love to the knitter forced itself into my mind and gave me a better picture of Tommy's wife than all his words had done. I felt my heart warm to her—to both of them, in fact—and a dimness came into my eyes which I had to wink away in order to see clearly.

The boys for'ard used to remark on the neatness and quality of Tommy's kit. For a bo'sun, he was particularly well-found. His underclothing especially—shirts, pants, socks, ties, etc., were all superfine and daintily made. Although an officer, he, like the rest of us, did his own washing, mending, ironing, darning, and so forth, and we commented on that, too. Not a stitch of his left the ship: everything was done by himself.

He wore a beautiful pair of sea-boots, fine, soft and yielding, which clung to his legs like stockings. I heard the gunners-mate say once that if he could find out where Tommy got them he would send to England for their double. But it seemed Tommy himself didn't know where they came from.

I now saw who was at the back of all this, and also the reason for the care and pride he took in his things. It was the thought of the loving hands of his wife around him; and for the first time in my life I realized what a powerful influence for good a devoted woman can be to the man who loves her.

While I was examining the gloves—one eye for them, the other squinting ahead—Tommy leaned partly over me, breathing hard. I gave a glance upwards and in the light of the binnacle caught a look of tenderness on his honest face that I would give worlds to be able to describe.

His face actually shone, while his eyes seemed to swim in moisture. A great gulp came into my own throat, which I was struggling hard to fight down, when a big wet splash fell on his bare hand and set me bubbling outright.

"Heavens!" I thought, with my heart bursting, "Tommy's crying!" and out welled the tear of sympathy. Tommy's glistened in the feeble light for the merest fraction of a second, then he shook it off, gave a heavy, choking sob, patted me on the shoulder, murmuring "It's all right, Jock. It's all right—tch, tch!" and went groaning over to the ship's side.

THE PENGUINS

Now I must make a little digression here: you will see the reason for it presently.

As I told you, we were on our way from the Falkland Islands back to Monte Video, where we expected soon to get our orders for home. At the last port of call, I forget the name of the place, the first lieutenant had had half a dozen penguins brought aboard for him. Great birds they were, as solemn as church-deacons and as round-paunched as bishops, with glittering eyes and long, hooked bills. A pair of bony-looking flippers hung from their sides, and they had splay, web feet, and walked with the motion of old women going to market.

These brutes were allowed to waddle about the deck at their own sweet will; and a downright nuisance they were, being in everybody's way. And couldn't they bite—and give you a wallop with their flippers! . . . My word! I tell you. you had to stand clear of them. If you made to push them gently out of the road with your foot—you daren't use your hand!—the beggars would grab at your leg and almost take the bit out if they caught you. If you happened to be lying under a sail taking a snooze during your watch on deck, and your feet worked loose, along would wobble one of these pirates and without the least warning clip a couple of your toes off if you weren't quick. It was nothing unusual to hear a yell in the dark, and have a man plunge in under the fo'c'sle lamp with his feet bleeding. We complained over and over again about them, but it was of no use. They belonged to Billy. That was enough.

No doubt they were fine birds to look at—lovely, soft-headed, black and grey plumage, downy breasts and a white patch on the head—one had a tuft on him like a hussar's bush. It was a treat to watch them ashore. You would see them standing in line—hundreds of them "dressed" and "eyes front "like soldiers, with the king penguin at their head. Then, you would think at a given signal, the whole squad would step out at once, waddle down the beach, dive into the sea and come up perhaps half a mile out all in line still.

I once saw a fight between two penguins for a fish. The one who had caught the fish was much smaller than the other, and the big one tumbled the little one over a great many times, first this way then that, for all the world like an Aunt Sally, but the wee one stuck to his guns and eventually carried off the prize. They're harmless enough in their own element and, I believe, kept by themselves in the ship, might have been interesting shipmates, like the turtles and the parrots and other pets the ship was full of. But not roaming wild, oh, no!

Anyway, this night, after Tommy regained his composure and began talking again, I fancied I saw, with the tail of my eye, a something move in the black shadow thrown by the bulwarks—a sort of blacker smudge.

But the bo'sun did not see it, and I was much too interested in what he was saying, and in the steering of the ship, and in the romance of the hour to take particular notice. Under that glittering canopy, with no sound striking the ear but the swish of the water rushing past the bows, or the creak of mast and spar, or perhaps the harsh croak of some passing albatross; and no motion but the lift and fall of the sails, and the "keek" of the star round the leech, all this was of far too much interest for me to bother about other things.

Tommy was telling me his love story!

A Sailor's Wife

In glowing words, and a low voice, musical as a 'cello, he pictured his wife as only a sailor, forcibly separated and condemned to a long exile from the girl of his heart, can picture her.

He told me how he had met her at a Naval ball in Dover and fallen instantly in love with her, and she with him. It was a case of love at first sight. He couldn't account for it, could never have conceived such luck would come his way. . . . A well-educated girl—was a teacher in one of the high-schools there. . . . And such a sweet little thing!—eyes blue, sunny golden hair, and such a smile! The sun in the tropics nothing to it . . . dazzling! . . . When he stood up and stretched out his arm she could stand comfortably under it, and lay her head in his arm-pit. . . . He could feel it now! . . . He could lift her and set her on his shoulder as easily as a baby. . . . And laugh! . . . She was always laughing . . . always laughing and singing . . . "the blithest, sweetest, daintiest little lark ever formed by Creation." These were his very words. God damn the unfeeling devils at the Admiralty for tearing him away from her! . .

"And, d'ye know, Jock, we've such a nice little house on the Dover cliff overlooking the Channel. There's a trim pailing in front—I painted it—green—before I came away. . . . A bit of garden, and a shell-covered path right up to the door, which has a brass knocker—a figure of the great Lord Nelson—the quaintest gadget you ever clapt eyes on. And the house is furnished in proper style—her father came out strong there. He's a retired matey from Portsmouth yard, y'know, but belongs to Dover. I don't like dockyard mateys as a rule, but he's the exception—a rare sort. He's with her now—being taken care of, bless her!

"And there she rules, queen of the hive, and every- body loves her!

D'ye know, while you and I are talking" (he was doing it all himself! I hadn't spoken a word. I wouldn't have interrupted him for a year's pay.) D'ye know, while you and I are talking, she'll p'raps be sitting in the parlour knitting or sewing or doing some of those things which females love to occupy their time with, singing, of course, and thinking . . . thinking. . . . Oh! I know what she'll be thinking about. . . .

"She puts a light in the window every night; she told me she would. . . . And my slippers are always ready waiting for me to put 'em on. . . . And everything ship-shape and sailor fashion. . . . Ah, she's a dear little girl! I've a photograph of her down below in the cabin, Jock; I'll show you it someday. . . .

"D'ye know what I'll do when I get home? . . . I'll take her by surprise. . . . I'll steal up the path, at knock the door quietly, and wait. . . . Then she'll to come the door. . . . I'll open my arms, and——

"Hell and damnation!" he cried, breaking off suddenly, and kicking out with both feet. . . . "What the devil's that! . . . Something has bit me! . . . D'ye see anything? . . . Mind your course! . . . Holy sailor, what can it be? . . ."

The pauses were filled up with hops and curses. Never in all my life was I so startled. For the moment I almost lost the power of my limbs. Luckily, the instinct of a sailor enabled me to keep the ship straight and prevent an accident. When I got the star into position again I looked around and saw a dark object waddling away towards the main mast. Meanwhile, Tommy had hopped, cursing all the way, round the wardroom hatch and unshipped the port binnacle light.

"It's one of those penguins, sir," I said.

"Oh, is it!" he growled. "Is that what it is? . . . Blast me if he hasn't gone through my trousers, sea-boot and all, right through to my leg, damn him! Look at that!"

He held the light to his leg and I looked. It was right enough. A rip about half an inch long was torn in the fine leather.

What the bo'sun said when he saw that hole I leave the reader to imagine. It would be a shame to ask any decent comp. to set it up. But I peered over to where Mr. Penguin was moving about and said to myself: "My boy, there's a funny five minutes in store for you very shortly!"

I looked at my little guide to see how she was taking the turn of events. She was twinkling away as happy as a sand-girl, and enjoying the situation prime, seemingly. She would see relief in store for us!

Tommy shipped the light again, after rubbing his leg, and was turning down his trousers, when I hissed: "Here, he's coming out again, sir!"

"Oh, is he? All right. . . . You hol' on a bit. . . . I'll fix him in a minute."

Between the two binnacles was the standard compass, a column-like erection standing about seven feet high. Here Mr. Baynham took his sights and "made" eight bells every day at noon. The compass was reached by a couple of little ladders, and there was a hinged flap which, when turned up, formed a platform. This flap hung down when not in use, and the opening between the standing part of the platform and the flap was filled with a stout piece of elm carved to resemble a rope.

Tommy unshipped this weapon and I, admiring his resource as he passed between me and the binnacle, whispered: "There he is, sir: d'ye see him? Just by the engine-room hatch. He's coming for another taste."

"By Jehu he'll get one!" muttered the bo'sun, seemingly from behind clenched teeth. "I see the devil. . . . Wait till he comes a bit closer."

He edged off a little to give himself more elbow-room, and the "shape," barely discernible on the dark deck, hobbled nearer and nearer.

Then Tommy took a spring. There was a dull thud, as if a bag of flour had been struck in the middle; a hoarse "quack"; a splutter in the mizzen rigging; then another gurgling "qu-a-a-a-e-e-kl"; the fall of a heavy body, and "all was still," as the poet says.

"Got him all right, eh ?" said Tommy, in a tone of triumph. "Gave him a lift in the world for once in his life, the bow-wow pirate! *He* won't trouble us any more, I'll be bound."

He then replaced the piece of wood, and saying he would take a look round, went off, leaving me to grin up to my star and think over the events of the night.

But the bo'sun was wrong. Our troubles were not all over yet. He had not been gone more than five minutes, and I was whistling softly to myself:

A sailor's wife a sailor's star shall be,
Yo, ho, we go across the sea! . . . .

when another hullabaloo broke out, this time in the cabin, and the captain came rushing out in his pyjamas, shouting for the officer of the watch.

177

It turned out that the skipper, being fond of air, had given orders for the cabin skylight to be left open, and the penguin had tumbled right through it, and in some way got to the captain's bed and given him a nip and woke him up.

Wasn't there a row!

Tommy seized the bird, and with one swing sent it whirling over the side about twenty yards before it struck water.

The skipper's arm was scratched, and there was a terrible to-do about it. Fancy biting the sacred flesh of the captain! The thing was without precedent. Nearly all hands were roused by the commotion.

The captain sharply questioned the bo'sun as to how the penguin got there, but Tommy, foreseeing no end of explanations, and perhaps scenting danger to himself, wisely held his tongue. Naturally, I took my cue from him and said nothing.

Next day orders came for'ard that all the penguins were to be thrown overboard. Curly Millet told us the skipper had given Billy a proper talking-to, and said some very pretty things about the men's comfort, and their home-life being interfered with, and so forth.

Here's one of the captain's paragraphs, spouted to us by Curly—he imitating the skipper by stumping about the deck to give it effect:

"Damn it, sir, these birds are a grievance, a-a-positive affliction. Not only an affliction, sir, but an infliction—a menace to the men! I cannot have the peace of the ship disturbed by vicious, rampaging creatures of that description prowling around. Overboard they must go, and at once!"

And so the ship rejoiced. Billy was a selfish sort of skunk; never bothered about anybody but himself, so there was little sympathy for him.

Tommy afterwards showed me his wife's portrait, and a sweet little lady she looked. He also gave me his address, and invited me to drop in upon them if I ever happened to be in their part of the world, but alas! that well-intentioned visit never came off.

Many a "crack" I had with him afterwards, and always found him a rare, congenial soul. Certainly he swore a good deal—sometimes, indeed, when he was angry he did nothing else. But to hear him at church service of a Sunday, joining in the singing (he was a Plymouth Brother, one of the most tolerant, broadminded of the sect I ever met), his deep bass voice coming thump! thump! like the pedal-notes of the organ, and his face a study in devotional rapture, you would have thought him a saint.

And I would sooner have Tommy for a mate than some of the oily, holy people I have been shipmates with, both at sea and ashore. These gentry always remind you of a gem with too much polish. Tommy was eighteen carat all through—a proper rough diamond.

Whether he went home and surprised his wife as he said he would I never knew. Anyhow, I hope he is still alive, with a crowd of "bairn's bairns" romping round his knee, and "cuddling his auld grey hairs."

If he is gone—peace to his ashes!

CHAPTER 26

The Swallow How to Catch Monkeys

Do you know how to catch monkeys? No? Then come along, and I'll show you how it's done in the forests of South Brazil.

After we came back from the Falklands, we lay at Monte Video for a fortnight or so refitting and painting ship, and then took a trip up the coast of Uruguay.

We had called in at one of those desolate, outlandish places we were forever touching at in our "shopping expeditions," as we called them; where we dropped anchor, sent a boat ashore, did something, and then up anchor and away again.

I don't remember the exact locality. Somewhere N. of Uruguay, between Rio de Janeiro and the Rio Grande. But it really doesn't matter. Indeed, these calls were so little thought of that scores of them are not even marked on the chart.

A more dreary, God-forsaken place you couldn't imagine. Where we lay, you seemed to be sitting in the pit of the theatre looking on to a dark forest scene. A big bite seemed to have been taken out of the land by one of those long, spoon-like mouths that only dentists are familiar with, leaving an expanse of dark, mysterious water, deeper than a bay but not deep enough to be called a gulf, down to the very verge of which came the trees in great serried rows, like an immense army.

On this sheet of water sat the *Swallow*, like a little homer-pigeon resting on her way home. To the right of us trees, trees, trees for miles and miles; to the left the same. In front, or rather in line with the port cathead, was a little piece of gleaming white pebbly beach, and a few ramshackle huts—showing that the place wasn't *man*-forsaken anyhow. I wondered to myself how men could possibly live in such a place, but never thought I should go ashore and see how pleasantly life can be made to pass even in a forlorn, out-of-the-way corner like that.

We arrived there one morning shortly after breakfast. About seven bells in the forenoon watch (half-past eleven), two men came aboard in a little canoe, asking for some sugar bags. They had the flat-headed look of the Indian, but spoke English well enough to be understood, and seemed intelligent fellows. They said they were willing to pay for whatever bags might be given them, and spoke so deferentially to the first lieutenant, who was standing beside the gangway when they came aboard, and looked so good-natured, that he called the steward, and told him to see them supplied. Tall, sinewy men they were, with copper-coloured faces; dressed in a sort of blouse with no sleeves (just a piece of cloth, like thin blue flannel, with a hole for the head to go through, and held together with a leather thong), and light skin leggings and *moccasins*.

While they waited, "Cooks" went (the dinner bugle), so we took them below and shared our dinner with them. One came to our mess, and I sat beside him. He told us that he and his mate were trappers and hunters. There were others ashore, he said; those were their houses we saw from the ship; their wives and little ones were there. Just now they were on a monkey hunt: that was what they wanted the bags for.

Suddenly, while he ate, he turned to me and put the question I have addressed to you at the top of this chapter. And I answered him exactly as I daresay you would answer me now: "No," shaking my head and smiling.

"Ah! that peety. . . . Heem good. . . . Fonnyl . . . You make him dronk," he said, imitating the gait of a staggering man. "Suppose you shoot. . . . Then you keel heem, or hort heem. He no good—'less you want to eat heem," he said hastily. "Oh yes. Then he plenty good—Ah!" he smacked his lips. (I thought of our Jacko, and wondered who would care about eating him!) "But you make heem dronk—ah. *Then* you catch heem. . . . No other way, no!"

My chum, Jack, who was sitting on my other side, nudged me—"That would be worth seeing, Jock."

"Yes," said the Indian. "Good! . . . Fonny, oh fonny! Plenty round here. . . . You come along with us. We show you. Not far away. One half hour."

"Oh! shouldn't I like to!" I said.

I hurried up with my dinner and went on deck, wondering if it would be possible to get an afternoon ashore. I looked along the starboard side. Nobody there but Spotty, the marine, on sentry at the cabin door. Spotty, however, seeing me, inclined his head slightly to port, as much as to say "He's over there." So I crossed the deck and, to my joy, there was Mr. Routh taking his midday smoke in the waist.

I had no fear of him, so up I goes, and, saluting, said: "Beg pardon, sir; but are we going to lie here long?"

"I couldn't say, Noble: about a week, at least," he replied.; The doctor and Baynham and I are going for a day's shooting when we can get it arranged, and we'll need some of you fellows with us."

I grinned. Those outings with Routh were great things, and all hands were ready to jump whenever he held up his finger. Half a dozen of us had once been on a rhinoceros hunt with him up the Niger, and the memory of that glorious day began to work in me. I remember it still, and see him now leaning against the gangway puffing leisurely at his pipe. I had half a mind to try and book a seat in advance, as the saying is, but held back, reflecting that that would not be fair to the other fellows, and for fear he might think I was currying favour. So I just grinned and told him about the trappers we had below, and what they were going to do; finishing up by asking if he thought there would be any chance of getting ashore with them to see the sport.

He didn't think there would be any objection to that. Only the captain's permission would be needed. In the meantime he would speak to Billy. Said he: "You go below, find out how many want to go ashore, then one of you come aft and make your request to Mr. Daniells. He'll put you all right."

"Thank you, sir, very much!" said I, and ran across the deck so that I could get kicking my heels together, and cutting a caper or two without his seeing me. But Spotty saw, and his eyebrows went up to the top of his head wondering what was in the wind. Spotty was a solemn sort of shipmate and I daresay thought I was cracked, especially as I executed a whirligig with both legs for his own particular benefit, before diving below.

Here, the Indians had finished dinner and were sitting on the gunner's chest with a bundle of bread bags between them. One was leaning against the ventilator, playing a lively air upon a pipe made of bamboo—a double-jointed instrument, something of a cross between a clarionette and a chanter—which he took to pieces and carried in his blouse—the other, bent forward, was performing a regular "brudder bones" accompaniment on the chest.

I couldn't understand how this chap produced such a rattle till I looked at his fingers and saw they were sheathed in little thimble-like contrivances made of hard hide or bone. The music was thin and reedy, but very pleasant. A basin with some grog in it stood in front of them, and the pair, smiling like seraphs, were playing away for all they were worth, while our fellows were gathered round in a state of enchantment.

I waited till the tune was finished, and then made known my interview with Mr. Routh. At this there was a kick-up, for of course everybody wanted to go with him. But the question was—who wanted to go with the Indians? A good many would have liked this too, but when it was pointed out that whoever went "monkeying" would very likely lose the chance of going with Routh, the crowd dwindled down to four—Jack, my chum, Shortie Edwards, Josie Deakin and myself.

This settled, I was chosen to state the case to Billy, and went aft. There was no trouble whatever. Routh had paved the way, bless him! In five minutes I was back with the skipper's permission. In five more the four of us were in the cutter, and within twenty, from the time the suggestion was first made (our Indians having asked us to wait while they got their things together), I was standing on the beach looking at the prettiest picture my eyes delighted to rest on—the *Swallow*, with the sunshine all about her, sitting like a little jewelled toy on an oblong mirror under a crystal dome.

From here the scene was even more impressive than when viewed from the ship. To right and left the great trees rising tier on tier like mighty giants, making men look such puny, puny objects beside them. The thick undergrowth. The strange creepers twining around every other tree, some as thick as a man's wrist, some like whipcord and about as tough. The wonderful glossy greenness of the leaves, which were of all shapes and forms, and of all shades and tints—some long and narrow, some broad, some almost round, hanging from a stem like a thread. The vast sheet of water glittering now with the sun upon it; the land, with every object it contained, mirrored seemingly thousands of feet beneath its motionless surface. Not a bird was in sight. Not a sign of life anywhere, except the light plume of smoke rising from the ship's funnel. The ship herself, the only relieving object in all that wide expanse, and she the dantiest little thing you could think of, the trucks at her mast heads shining like gold buttons, their photographs twinkling far below as merrily as did the real ones aloft.

I have never forgotten that picture. From where I stood you seemed

183

to be in front of a great bay window gazing into eternity, and the *Swallow* the vehicle whose destiny it was to take you there. A sweeter conveyance you couldn't have wished for.

I looked at her with loving affection! There she lay like a sweet little poem in cordage and timber with everything bright and sparkling about her. For nearly three years and a half she had been my home. I knew every plank, rope, spar and stanchion aboard of her. The little bird at her bow was the most beautiful thing in all the world to me. I could have taken it down, carried it home, set it up among my humble household gods, in much the same spirit as a Chinaman sets up his Joss, to be an object of veneration forever. It would have recalled my happiest hours. I could see the two scuttles that bounded my daily horizon, marking the place where I ate, drank, slept and lived my life. And a fine life it had been—some days, truth to tell, anything but pleasant, but who thinks of trifles at such a moment!

I loved my little ship. And I love her still. Looking through a "lang luk" of years crammed full of real troubles—things that harass the soul of a man—I recall nothing but comfort, happiness and good-fellowship from the day I joined till the day I payed off from her.

However, to my tale. I turned, with eyes full of mist, and looked at the houses behind. They were poor erections, if you like. Just branches of trees laid one on top of the other; not nailed, but tied together with creepers, and covered with leaves.

Some brown-skinned children, as naked as Nature had turned them out, were playing around; and two women, naked also to the waist, were busy over two different fires cooking something in jar-like vessels which hung from tripods made of bent saplings and tied at the top with creepers. These creepers seemed to be a very useful adjunct to the camp, for I saw the family washing suspended between two huts and it was a creeper that was doing duty as a clothes-line.

The whole place reminded one of nothing so much as a gipsy encampment. Somebody was thrumming a guitar or banjo behind the hut facing us, the sound rising clear in the air like a bell. We heard also the squeal of a pipe like the one our friend had been playing aboard, and were edging nearer, to get a view of the performers, when the man himself popped round the corner and beckoned to us to come over.

Behind this hut was a piece of sward bare of trees, save for one in the centre, which had a trunk as round as our capstan, and a top like an umbrella, the branches covering the whole camp. Here a few more kiddies were romping about. A number of men and women, brown-skinned, and naked, except for loin cloths, sat or stood on the grass, while two men with their backs against the tree discoursed music: one from a pipe such as I've already described, the other from a three-stringed instrument made out of half a dried gourd.

In front of the musicians two little girls were being taught to dance by a very fat woman who, with gleaming eyes and teeth, squatted tailor-fashion a little to the left clapping her hands and shouting directions to them. The people around were all seemingly as interested in the performance as the youngsters themselves, who skipped and twisted about as if they were on wires. This woman didn't clap her hands in the prim way we do, but made her whole body go—elbows, shoulders, head, every muscle of her massive bulk heaving in time to the beat.

One glance was enough to tell how keenly *she* was interested. Her heavy breasts hung in front of her like bladders, and her whole body glistened with sweat from the exertions she was making. But if ever a human face spoke of a glad heart, that woman's did. It simply beamed. In fact, everybody around the tree looked happy. I thought it a gay scene. But we hadn't time to look at it. The moment we hove in sight the children ran screaming to the huts, the women after them; the musicians jumped to their feet and skipped behind the tree, the whole scene dissolving like a cloud in a midsummer sky. Even now I can see the instructress roll on to her hands and feet and go bounding over the grass as if Old Nick himself were after her.

You couldn't have helped laughing to save your life. All four of us were sorry to see the breakup of such a nice little scene, and tried to get them started again. But it was no good. So our friends the trappers, joined by three of their mates carrying the bags and other parcels, one with a long weapon like a bill hook, which was used for cutting a way through the undergrowth, told us to come along, and off we struck into the forest.

After a march of about three-quarters of an hour, we came to a wide clearing, so suddenly that it was as if you had opened the door in a house and stepped into the street. One minute you were in the semi-darkness of the forest, the next in broad daylight. Here there were nothing but stumps of trees, around the roots and mounds of which grew the strangest-looking flowers I ever saw. Some gorgeously coloured, some delicately tinted, some so queerly shaped that, to me, they looked like huge, wonderfully-formed insects stuck on wires for exhibition, like you often see in the museums or in milliners' shop-windows.

All around were trees, mighty erections towering over a hundred feet high, with others, as big as the ones we have in Scotland, growing beneath them. Some of these trees must have been over a thousand years old. Great gnarled monsters standing twelve or fourteen feet thick and as firm as castles, their leaves as fresh and glossy and healthy as the hair on a young girl's head. I remember thinking to myself as I stood looking at them, "Lord! who was on the earth when *you* first took root? ... And yet you look as if you had another thousand years of life in you, and even then wouldn't be used up—green and hearty still!" Dear, dear!

Man is called the "Lord of Creation," but what a poor, insignificant, transitory thing he is when put alongside other works of the Divine Architect! These things make you think big! I don't wonder at travellers, tramps and sailors, being men of large mind.

Right round the clearing you could hear the monkeys chattering as if you had come into a city full of them. They were quite near, we could see them skipping about among the branches all around. Thousands of parrots, too, were in evidence, both to the sight and hearing.

As we came along we had been hearing them, but here the noise was worse than in a bird-shop. Also, as we came through the forest, when a break occurred in the dense canopy above, we had seen gaily-plumaged birds float by, and lovely hanging plants, and vines loaded with grapes, but not ripe enough for eating. We came upon a whole grove of limes, the yellow fruit glistening high overhead; another of pomegranates; and saw the myrtle in its beauty, and the palm, and the pine, and the coconut and the lovely cedar and the wide-spreading cork tree. But we heard no singing birds. Nature seems to have expended all her art on the plumage out there, and *that* beggars description.

We saw jays and woodpeckers by the score; birds with long, shining tails, stars on their wings, glittering top-knots, and all sorts of decorations. Parrots whose raiment outdid in splendour the most gorgeous uniform ever seen on earth. Beautiful little humming-birds, but no songsters. I don't remember hearing anything like our blackbird, or mavis, or lark, for instance. It was all display and no music. Once or twice we heard the bell-bird, but you wouldn't call his note a song. Although you could hear it a long distance away it was more like the creak of a dry axle. But we caught no glimpse of him, much as I should have liked to.

Better guides, or more congenial mates than those Indians, you couldn't have wished for. They didn't know what to do to repay our kindness to them on board the ship. They made as much of that as if we had spread a banquet for them, and entertained the whole camp. Everything likely to interest us they pointed out; the birds, the flowers, the trees, naming them, and telling us about them and about the nature and habits of the wild animals which were lurking around, hidden, but watching us all the same. They seemed as familiar with the forest as we were with the ship.

One of the men, who carried a bow and arrows, brought down a large bird, like a pheasant, and hung it on the bole of a mighty beech, with the remark that we would get it on our way back. But we didn't. When we returned we got the skeleton of that bird picked as clean as though there had never been flesh on it at all. Some hawk or vulture had got him. But we took the leathers aboard as a trophy. I kept one for years as a bookmark, till it wore away altogether.

Once, when we came to a slight opening on the top of a hill, which gave us a view of tree-tops, stretching seemingly to the world's end, they showed us the track of a fire which had cut I swath through the forest as wide as the Thames at the Nore Light. At another time, they pointed out the trail of a large animal, called a tapir, and showed us where he had stopped to scratch himself against a tree, and left some of his hair.

That walk through the wood I remember as well as though it happened the day before yesterday.

However, this was the end of it. Without more ado, the trapper who had sat beside me in the mess, and who seemed to be the master of ceremonies, threw down his bundle of bags, crying, "Ah! dis heem! ... Now de fon begeen. ... Look! See heem jomp!"

He led us into the centre of the clearing (the bow and arrows, and the bill-hook being first of all carefully hidden out of sight), the monkeys meanwhile skipping and chattering around us like a crowd of excited children at a fair. Here we all sat down on the grass in a circle like a picnic-party, and the parcels were opened. One man brought out a *calabash*, made from a flattened *gourd*, and covered with plaited straw (I saw a hot-water bottle just like it the other day). A little tumbler of the same material, only without the straw covering, was fitted over the cork. This *calabash* was filled with a native spirit—*Chakaça* they called it—brewed from sugar-cane, and pretty nearly as strong as our whisky.

Another produced some slabs of dried meat and a kind of biscuit, not unlike a "soda scone," both in shape and texture, but tasteless, it being baked without salt. Another, some tobacco. Another—this being one of the men who had sat with his back to the tree—his instrument, which, on a nearer view, I now saw to be a neat little contrivance like a mandoline, only crude and unpolished, with strings made of gut, or some such substance, instead of wire. There were also two pipers, and our friend with his bone thimbles.

When everything was ready, the M.C., as I may call him, sat down in the centre of the circle, telling us not to look around, but just watch the monkeys in front of us, as the least thing would frighten them all away. He then, with a great show and flourish, uncorked the calabash, poured some of the liquor into the tumbler, and handed it to one of his mates, who tossed it off, smacked his lips, rubbed his stomach, and then handed the tumbler back with the same display. This ceremony was repeated over and over again, till we had all had a glass each; then the M.C. took one himself and rubbed *his* stomach.

There was no hurry. We just sat talking and laughing, while the Indians told us little stories of former forays. We seemed a harmless party of humans resting in the woods, and thinking of nothing but our own enjoyment. This was really the trap set for Mr. Monkey, and wonderfully well it worked.

While all this was going on, the monkeys, thinking themselves unobserved, had stopped chattering, and come out to the extreme end of the branches to get a closer view of the proceedings. It was almost impossible to keep from laughing at the antics and grimaces of them. They were of all aces and sizes, from the hoary old patriarch, with a bald head and a beard like a goat's to the tiny little Jenny no bigger than a kitten. I don't know what species they belonged to—the Capuchin, I think—but I can tell you they were absolutely eaten up with curiosity; especially the younger ones. One little fellow, with a grey body, and a face like a gargoyle, almost fascinated me; he looked so hideous. Hanging by his tail, he swung out as far as he could, and seemed to devour us with his little sharp eyes.

Then the bread and meat was broken up and divided with the same elaborate parade, and another glass of Chakaça handed round. Then we got out our pipes, lit them, and the musicians tuned up. After this there were a few more rounds, and then, when the excitement in the trees seemed raised to fever-heat (although we appeared to be unaware of a monkey being within a hundred miles of us), our M.C. brought out a smaller *calabash*, holding about a pint of Chakaça, of a much stronger quality, and, while one of the others wrapped up the big one, he winked to us, and said, "Dis for heem. He good. Plenty ol' right now. Coom along."

At this we all got to our feet—the *calabash*, with the little tumbler beside it, the broken bread and meat, and a couple of smoking pipes were left on the ground—and, with the musicians leading and playing, we all went dancing back into the forest like a troop of wood- land elves.

I can see the bodies of the Indians swaying before me as I write, and the flap of Shortie's white duck bell-bottoms as the music lifts his heels. (Shortie, as you know, was a great dancer; and that day he wore an extra wide pair of trousers). I can also hear the M.C., as he stops piping for a moment, call over his shoulder, "No look! No look!" which we four, as full of the spirit of the hunt as himself, interpret as "Eyes front!" and go skipping after him like schoolboys playing a game. To this day, never a monkey do I see in the street but back comes the whole scene and I live over again that delightful afternoon.

When we got to where the bags had been left we drew up, and the M.C. cried, "Now look!—What I tell you? ... He fonny.... Good!"

The space we had vacated was black with moving bodies. A circle like our own was formed, with a big fellow in the centre, with a beard like Abraham, going through the motions of our master of ceremonies exactly as he did. Outside the circle, the monkeys were jumping, wriggling, falling over and on top of each other in a state of the wildest excitement. At one moment you could see nothing but whirling arms, legs, and waving tails; at another, out would shoot the long, lean body of the central figure, with the calabash in his hand, and the Chakaça squirting from it. And the noise! ... You never in all your life heard such a row. It was the most laughable sight I ever saw. Often and often I have thought what a rare touch a scene like this would make in a picture-film. We couldn't keep our eyes from it. But the Indians, who took it in the day's work, now set about getting out the bags, and laying them ready to hand. Then the M.C. came over to us and said—"What you tink: HeemGoodeh? ... Fonny? ... .Ah! . . . But," lifting his hands, "oh, no! Not near fonny enough! You wait . . . Bymby heem good; heep, heep good! ... Look how he jomp! Ol' right. We have jomp, too. Coom on!"

He then took out his pipe, set himself against a tree, struck up a soft, dreamy native waltz, gave a nod to his mates, who each came and took one of us for a partner, and away we went gliding over the short grass, as if life was a ballroom and we had nothing to do but dance.

The row in the open was like Bedlam let loose. All the monkeys in the world seemed to be there, and all yelling at once; while the parrots, thousands of whom were in the trees, and who love nothing better than a din, took up the chorus till the welkin rang with discordant cries. But the Indians never heeded. If you happened to catch the piper's eye, he just nodded at them and winked, as much as to say, "Heem Good!"

Then we had a *"cotillion"*—a square dance, like a quadrille—the Indians going through the measure first to show us the figure, singing as they went. It often amuses me to hear people say that Indians have no music in them. They can't mean Brazilian Indians. These people have the music of Old Castile, Italy, Sicily—all the tribes of Europe in their veins, and express it in every note of their voices; every twirl or twang of their instruments, every movement of their agile bodies. In Scotland we don't know how to sing. We are afraid to open our mouths in case somebody is looking. That's not the way abroad. There they are natural and spontaneous, and sing like birds and as loud as their lungs will let them.

The music for the *cotillion* I speak of is a light, airy, tripping measure. I brought it home with me, and during the last forty years have sung it to myself at least ten thousand times, making as many moments, which might otherwise have been dull, bright and happy. Only last year, no further gone, I gave it to a friend of mine (Mr. Knox Williamson), one of Ayr's most gifted musicians, to use in an operetta he was producing, where it made a decided "hit." Of course, I cannot give you the words the Indians sang to it, not knowing their language; but here is the last verse of a setting I made for myself, which has at least caught the spirit, and will give you an idea of the rhythm:

Oh, life is always sing-time
To those who know the tune,
And youth is happy spring-time
And fresh as flowers in June.
The heart that's blithe and merry
Keeps sweet the live-long day,
And never thinks to worry—
Then, let us all be gay!
Sing high, sing low—a fig for woe!

Be happy while you may!
Chorus:
Happy and merry, tra-la, la-la-la,
Happy and merry, tra-la, la-la-la,
Birds of the air are no freer than we are,
So happy and merry are we, ha! ha!

All this time (twenty minutes or so—half an hour at the most), it was Babel in the clearing, if not absolute pandemonium. The monkeys had started a free fight, and skin and hair were flying in handfuls! Our M.C. therefore stopped the music, unscrewed his pipe, put it away saying—"Now, I tink heem good. . . . Wait! . . . Now you see fon! . . ." He then nodded to the bowman, who picked up his bow and a couple of arrows. Then he divided the begs amongst us, two to each man, and we all crept to the edge of the clearing. Here I pause was made, and the M.C. whispered, "When I say 'Now!' all ron queek!" He then nodded again to the bowman, who stepped back a little, fitted a shaft and sent it flying into the writhing mass. "Now!" shouted the M.C, and into the open we bounded, whirling our bags and yelling like demons!

Then took place a scene that would baffle the pen of a Dickens to describe. The monkeys stopped their uproar on the instant; looked, for the moment, "too astounded for words," as the saying is, then went leaping, tumbling, somersaulting to the trees opposite like an army in panic, leaving about a dozen staggering on the grass like "drunks" on a Saturday night.

These, as we came near, assumed the most comical attitudes. Some showed their teeth; others swayed about and tried to look dignified; some were hilariously frisky; one I'm positively certain (and this is as true as I live), was trying to sing a song, and stood, with his arms waving, and his chest expanded, like an opera star. (You should have seen Josie imitating him later a-board the ship!) Indeed, they behaved just as tipsy men do, according to their natures, and looked so screamingly funny, that all four of us, who were seeing such a sight for the first time, were utterly helpless with laughing.

But the trappers soon made short work of them. They bundled them into the bags, and tied them up so quickly, that in five minutes the whole lot was disposed of. The old monkey, who had been their M.C., and who had imbibed "not wisely but too well," was found lying dead drunk, a most disreputable-looking object, with the *calabash* in one hand, and a pipe in the other. He was shorn of his honours, and left lying where he fell, being too heavy to carry, and too old for sale.

Two were killed by the arrow—actually skewered together, like pieces of beef ready for the pot. This the trappers told us, would please their wives, who were very fond of monkey. The arrow was not withdrawn from the bodies, but pushed farther in, and in this way they were carried back to the camp as a trophy.

There was great rejoicing when we arrived; the trappers congratulating themselves on their afternoon's work, and we on the fine outing we had enjoyed.

Two days afterwards the officers' hunt came off. But I missed it. The four who had been monkey-catching were barred. The party brought back a fine "bag"—the jolly-boat pretty nearly full of both fur and feather—the principal item being a big deer-like animal, called a guanaco, if I remember rightly—and said to be one of the unclean beasts that Noah took into the Ark with him. But, clean or unclean, its bones were well picked on board our ship, I tell you! And the officers were loud in praise of the Indians, who had made themselves very useful.

A great day, by all accounts. But I didn't grumble. You can't have everything in this world.

CHAPTER 27

Homeward Bound

One day, some weeks after coming back to Monte Video, I was standing at the fo'c'sle rail watching the gig, which was making for the steps in front of the Government Buildings, with the first lieutenant seated in the stern. There was a meeting of the big-wigs ashore, or a ball or function of some kind, which he was on his way to attend. It was a lovely day. The sun, shining as it *can* shine in the Argentine, lit up the dark brown waters of the La Platt, turning them into billows of molten copper. The town lay sweltering in the heat, with a soft haze hanging over it, like the gauzy "clouds" that overhang a scene in a theatre, while the windows in the house for which the boat was making seemed to have a sun of its own blazing behind the glass.

Billy was in full war-paint—cocked hat, epaulets, white gloves, sword, gold lace, cord and tassels galore, all of which the light struck in brilliant flashes, making a fine show. I thought, "If Billy could see himself today as we see him from the ship, my word, wouldn't he be a proud man!" The boat was painted white, with a gold band running along the gun'le beading, and this the sun also played with in merry twinkles as she went dancing over the water.

The crew were in white frocks and white straw hats. I knew them all. In fact, the whole boatload were the very men I had celebrated in song, as the saying is—Chatty Kinsell being especially chummy with me on account of his having got two verses to himself. And, although I was very well accustomed to pictures of that kind, I must say I felt my heart warm to this one. The graceful bodies bending to their work; the oars, lifting with the regularity of clock-beats, hanging feathered for a moment, then flashing forward again, with the water sparkling from the blades like crescents of glittering dewdrops; the bow-wave rising at every send of the boat like a little auburn curl on the forehead of a beautiful girl—wasn't that a picture to warm the heart of any sailor? I thought it was, and mine warmed accordingly. It glows now at the mere memory!

A little ahead, and to port of us, another gunboat lay moored, the flag of Spain floating from her spanker gaff like a gold leaf edged with crimson. One of her boats, similar to our own, with two glittering figures in her stern-sheets, was also making for the Government House steps, and I was wondering which of the two would land first when a slap on the back nearly knocked my cap overboard. I turned round angrily, and there was Jack Belton, my chum, "squaring off" and dancing in front of me like a jumping-jack.

"Jock, old son!" he cried, "What do you think? The orders for home are aboard, and our relief is exected to heave in sight any minute."

"How do you know?" I asked, staying the rush I had meant to make at him.

"Westwater told me, he has just come for'ard. Hip! hip! hooray!— Embrace, you burgoo-eating son of a gun!"

I ran at him, and we had a little set-to, then round the fo'c'sle we circled to a tune that was high in favour at the time, singing as we waltzed:

I want to go home to mamma,
I want to go home to mamma,
It's naughty, I say,
To keep me away
When I want to go home to mamma!

GOODBYE TO URUGUAY

Then there was a week of hurry and confusion. I don't remember saying goodbye to Dirty Dick, nor to Rodrigo, though I'm sure I did. Nor do I recall the arrival of the *Dwarf*, our relief, nor any of the bustle and preparation previous to starting on our journey home.

What memory shows me next is Jack standing on the fore royal truck, and myself on the main, with the lightning-conductor between my bare feet, both of us waving bouquets of flowers as the *Swallow* slowly steams out of the harbour. (Ah, there was no rheumatism in those days!)

The shore is lined with people, the water alive with boats come out to see us away, the ships around all dressed in gay bunting, as we are, and cheers resound on every side. As I look around, seeing the fluttering handkerchiefs and hearing the huzzas, I feel the thrill that

194

comes when friends part, certain never to meet again. I had had some fine times in that old Uruguayan city, and was sorry to leave it. Yet, not sorry either; after all *"there's no place like home."*

Then comes a blank, till one morning I was on the lookout, after being some weeks at sea. It was dark when I came on the fo'c'sle, but fine, calm weather, and the sky full of stars. We were under steam. The time was just before dawn. I tramped from cathead to cathead, busy with thought, pleasantly looking forward to the end of the commission, which we expected within the next month, if all went well.

I had saved a few pounds, not many, God wot! for my pay wasn't great, and I had left "halfpay" to my mother, but I had managed to scrape together about £12, and that seemed a big sum to me then—not a bad one yet!—and the thought of sharing it with her, and of all the lovely times ahead—eight whole weeks of them!—filled my mind with hopes like merrie dancers, and sent the first half hour of my trick flying as if it had wings.

"Aha, mitherie! Not long now!" I cried, as her sweet old face rose from the water, smiled up at me and then faded away again.

To and fro I stumped—fore and aft the starboard side, across the deck, fore and aft the port, then athwartships again, back and fore, up and down; sometimes jumping on the hencoops to get a higher view 7 , all the while humming a little song of my own, set to a tune that pleased me, entitled "Little Mother"—I had sent it to her some time before, and she had written telling me she had had it *Framed!*—and the thought of that, and all the love behind it working in me, made my heart happy.

And then the girl! When I thought of that sweet little damsel and of all the joys ahead along with her, I tell you I felt fine! I kicked up my heels and took a waltz around the fo'c'sle hugging myself and singing that dear little thing of Marchand's, who at that moment was lying snoring below like a porpoise:

Neath the old cabin thatch, which shelters the starling,
I kissed her and kissed her again and again,

and so on, only I made it:

My tender wee Peggy o' Bonnie Dundee!

Ah! it *is* pleasant to be coming home after four long, weary years of absence.

DAWN ON THE SEA

There's no time for thinking and anticipating, especially after a four years' separation, like an hour on the look-out on a dark night. This was an ideal night—or rather morning—and I was enjoying it.

The stars were blazing overhead like holes in a black curtain with a strong light behind it. There wasn't a breath of wind save what the ship was making. Nothing in sight but an occasional glimmer on the water telling of some fish either hunting or being hunted. Not a sound but the pulsing of the engines, and the musical purl of the bow-wave under my feet, which struck my ear like the tinkling murmur of a waterfall in a highland glen.

Presently I stopped dead before the fish davit and looked intently towards the east. Something was happening there—a softening of the darkness in that quarter. A flimsy, gassy-like vapour seemed to be rising from the sea. This spread, widened, mounted, turned a distinct grey, then gradually brightened. . . . I knew what it was now—"Daybreak, sir!" I cried, without turning my head.

"Ay, ay!" answered Mr. Freedie, who was officer of the watch.

The hush that was on everything before seemed now to deepen, the stars to glow without a twinkle, the bow-wave to drop its chatter, the very engines to cease their clamour for the time being. It was as if the whole universe was waiting with bated breath for something wonderful about to happen. Then a soft strain of music, unearthly in its sweetness, began to steal over the surface of the sea, and swell and mount till the whole world, you would have thought, was full of it, and that a myriad unseen voices were chanting the birth of morning; while up crept the radiance to starboard, slowly—slowly—slowly blotting out the stars on the eastern horizon. Then a line of silver appeared on the edge of the circle, and went jerking—jerking—jerking, farther and farther out, as if a hand were drawing it, but had to stop and change its position on account of the wideness of the sweeps, the centre broadening as the line extended. Then a ripple of golden fire ran along, taking the place of the silver line, then another and another, glittering and giving off the loveliest colours—mauve, saffron, green, blood-red, purple—all the shades and tints you could think of.

All this time, which was not long, the radiance first seen was mounting higher and higher, quenching more and more stars, till now on the starboard side a pearly haze hung over the sea, making it plainly visible, while on the port, all was black and the stars shining as brightly as ever.

Then a great assortment of vari-coloured rays, fan-shaped in formation, shot into the sky and went flaming about like giant search-

196

lights, and on the very rim of the sea appeared a tiny object, of vivid, quivering brightness, which peeped over the water, as if looking to see who was there; shone for a moment like the new gold ring on the dainty finger of a young bride; seemed to dilate; flung a broad beam over the bosom of the ocean, instantly transforming its dead, glassy surface into a thing of leaping life and beauty, and sending every star in the firmament to sleep at once, and then, with a bound you would have thought, out sprang the full sun: the whole sea jumping to meet him, her face dimpled with smiles of welcome and clapping her hands. The miracle of day was once more wrought.

The sun brought a freshness with him that tasted like champagne, creating an appetite worthy of a far better breakfast than was our lot that glorious morning—a basin of greasy ship's cocoa, and a couple of hard biscuits. But just before "Cooks" went, a fine breeze came on from the Sou'west, which put the kybosh on "Old King Coal," and sent us spinning home with white wings and joyful hearts, thinking about bacon and eggs, morning rolls, butter, jam and all the other dainties that landsmen revel in, but which sailors in my time could lick their lips over only in imagination for months at a stretch. Still, God was good, and our time was coming!

Cloud Photography: A Camera "Effect"

This breeze brought us right up to Fayal, where we put in for letters. Here a little incident occurred which has stuck to my memory like a limpet.

A few of us had gone ashore for a leg-stretcher and climbed one of the mountain peaks. When we got to the top and looked around, a ring of soft, billowy cloud had encircled the hill a little way down and blotted out the bay. We could see over it right out to the horizon, but the water below and the town were completely hidden. The cloud was snow-white and as dense as wool. As we looked, it began to rise and come nearer to us, and then gradually to get thinner, and fade and fade away till it had no more substance than a lady's veil. Then out popped the ship, bottom up! Then the town, with its queer-looking houses, the trees around, the blue, sparkling water—the whole scene, in fact, spread itself out on that cloud and we had the sweetest little miniature picture before us you could imagine.

It seemed a hundred miles away. It was like looking through the big end of a telescope: every object far away, but clear and distinct. The only difference was that everything appeared upside down exactly as a picture looks when you see it through a camera. It was no optical illusion of mine. Every one of us saw it and stood spellbound till it vanished and things took their natural shape. It caused no end of talk. I spoke to Mr. Routh about it, and he said it was just an atmospheric effect like a mirage, but how it was brought about he knew no more than I did.

Home!

From Fayal to the neighbourhood of Cape Ushant it was sunny seas and laughing breezes all the way. The little *Swallow* under all possible sail, every rope taut, and straining every pinion, bounded over the wave-crests like a bird to its nest. You would have thought she knew she was going home. Sometimes she did her twelve knots, sometimes more, and kept it up for hours at a time. Then we would frisk about the fo'c'sle, slap the rail, jump under the bowsprit, pat her pretty head and call her all the endearing names we could think of—"Bonnie little bird!" "Good old girl!" "Darling *Swallow*—show 'em how you do it!" just to liven her up and keep her going. And she responded like a live thing.

It was lovely to see her. Dressed in gleaming white canvas, her graceful body rising and falling with the heave and swell, the waves dancing about her, and the long wake broadening out astern, she must have looked the prettiest little picture floating on the sea. On moonlight nights, as she swam along with her shadow thrown on the water, I used to stare at it for hours, thinking that no sight in the world could compare with this. That was one of the finest trips we had. I remember it well.

Soon we sighted Land's End, made our number, and ran into more muck—"proper Channel weather," as it is called. A regular gale was howling around the Cornish Coast. Here we came upon signals of distress from a sloop which was driven ashore, and landed our lifeboat just in time to snatch a baby about six weeks old from the very jaws of death. It was wrapped in shawls and an oilskin, and tightly pressed in its mother's arms. She, poor thing, was beaten to pulp on the rocks; but the baby was alive. They hadn't been long in the water. The sloop was knocked to pieces. Nobody could tell who she was or where she had come from. Everyone on board of her was drowned except the baby. *She*, the people ashore took charge of, and if she be alive now will be a woman well on in years.

Two days afterwards we dropped anchor at Spithead, and were

inspected by Captain Seymour. Then it was out powder and shot; into dock; dismantle, and—hey for Bonnie Scotland!

All about coming into Pompey Harbour, under steam, and with the long-commission pennant with a gilded balloon at the end of it streaming tar behind lit; the *St. Vincent's* band playing us in; the making fast to the buoy —the same buoy we had left from four years ago exactly to the day the fortnight in the dockyard; the yarns around the galley tire; the high jinks in the town during that fortnight—for your Homeward-bounder in from a long commission is always sure of a warm welcome!—the journey to Dundee— these are memories that will never fade, but would almost need a book for themselves.

I brought home a parrot (in a gorgeous cage which I had bought in London), a Spanish cardinal, two love-birds, a piece of the True Cross (purchased from a lying Maltee in Cape Town), a pair of horns from Uruguay, and some other little knick-knacks.

As the train drew up at Dundee the first face I saw was my mother's. And yet I hardly knew her, she had altered so much and seemed to have grown so small! She was the only soul I knew in all the crowd. I nearly jumped through the carriage window to get hold of her! . . .Ah, these mothers!

At the station gate (the railway landing-stage wasn't the elaborate thing then that it is now), standing by the kerb, a blind fiddler was scraping out "Home, Sweet Home" on his crazy old fiddle. I put my hand in my pocket meaning to give him tuppence. But happening to look at the coins before I dropped them in his little tin, I saw they were two two-shilling pieces. I hadn't the heart to draw back. I said to myself—

"Ah, well. Poor old chap. If they do you as much good as your wheezy old tune has done me—we're quits!"

Having bundled my belongings to the street, we were surrounded by cabmen yelling for custom. But there was to be no cabs for me that day. I was for marching home in state! So I hung the horns round my neck; swung my bag and ditty-box over my right shoulder, with the other trophies done up in a black silk handkerchief in the crook of my arm; hooked my fingers in the ring of the cage containing the cardinal and the two love-birds, and, my mother having taken the parrot to carry, I tucked her right under my left, and out we set.

It was a glorious June day, and there were lots of people about, and we had "*more spyers than buyers,*" as the saying is, but a happier pair than my old mother and I would have been hard to find, you may take my word for that!

And so ended half a dozen of the most helpful and happy years a young man could live, and practically finished my career in the Navy, for within little more than another I was hurt and—but that's a different story.